places

places

from the pages of the *new zealand listener*

A catalogue record for this book is available from the National Library of New Zealand

A RANDOM HOUSE BOOK
published by Random House New Zealand
18 Poland Road, Glenfield, Auckland, New Zealand

www.randomhouse.co.nz

First published 2005

© New Zealand Magazines 2005

The moral rights of the author have been asserted

ISBN 1-86941-755-0

Design by Nick Turzynski, redinc., Auckland

Front cover image: Okarito by Bruce Foster
Back cover image: Coromandel by Bruce Connew

Printed in China

contents

introduction

For 66 years the *New Zealand Listener* has sought to hold a mirror up to New Zealand, so that New Zealanders might see themselves and their country reflected back at them every week. Whatever the subject—politics, social issues, work or play—the *Listener* has gone behind the daily headlines to get the fuller story. For a truly national magazine, this does not mean doing it all from Auckland and Wellington. Since the earliest issues *Listener* writers and contributors have travelled to every corner of the country at some time or other, not necessarily to cover topical events but often simply to look at how life is lived and tell the rest of us about it.

This book features a wide selection of those stories, in both time and place, and a glance at the contents page indicates just how diverse they are. We go from deepest Fiordland in 1948 to Kaikohe in 2002; from the Helensville A&P show in 1977 to the Selwyn river in 2004. It's not all paddocks and bush by any means, though; not only do we take a stroll past the fleshpots of Karangahape Rd in central Auckland but we boldly go where strong men might quail to enter: a student hostel in Wellington and the living horror of Dunedin's scarfie flats.

Many of the articles are by staff writers such as Bruce Ansley, who has the covered the South Island for the *Listener* for 25 years, but there are also contributions by noted authors like Fiona Kidman (the Chatham Islands), Bruce Mason (Christchurch Town Hall) and "Sundowner", aka the magazine's pioneering editor, Oliver Duff.

Taken individually or together, these differing pieces form a vivid picture of New Zealand life, particularly over the past 30 years. Not the whole picture, by any means, but a rich and engaging one. There is something of all of us in here.

Denis Welch

Only Four Found
in 100 Years

10 december 1948

The fact that the notornis, generally considered by ornithologists to be about as dead as the dodo, is still living and apparently flourishing in the Fiordland district has excited natural history students and brought not a little fame to Dr Geoffrey Orbell, of Invercargill. Scientists far beyond New Zealand will be affected in one way or another by this reappearance of a bird which up till 1898 had been seen only four times.

It is heavier and more sturdily built than the familiar pukeko, and has shorter, stronger legs. But it also has the white under coverts of the tail which the pukeko flashes. The colour of the plumage varies according to the light and to the angle of view. Seen from the front, there are shades of bronze-green and indigo-blue with a bright sheen. Besides the mounted specimen in the Otago Museum, there are two skins in the British Museum. A third was sold in London to a representative of the Dresden Museum (Germany), but according to reports that museum, along with several others, was wiped out during the war, so it is unlikely that this specimen still exists.

The story of New Zealand's most uncommon and elusive bird is a fascinating one to Dr R. A. Falla, Director of the Dominion Museum. It must be equally intriguing to many other people, for during an hour-and-a-half's talk with *The Listener* about the notornis, Dr Falla's telephone rang a number of times, and each time the subject was the notornis.

The 'takahe party', from left: Joan Telfer, Rex Watson, Dr D. Jennings, Dr R. A. Falla, Neil McCrostie, Dr G. Orbell.

'It is always a matter of the greatest interest when ancient bird fauna are re-discovered.'

'It is always a matter of the greatest interest when ancient bird fauna (giant geese, rails and other birds smaller than the moa) are re-discovered,' said Dr. Falla. 'In a hundred years, up to the time of Dr. Orbell's discoveries, only four individual notornis have been found alive. It is true that in the long intervals between these encounters, competent observers such as surveyors, explorers and others, have reported seeing the famous bird, but in many cases their reports were not completely convincing. In 1924 a party traversing the Milford Track gave a circumstantial account of seeing a notornis, but their descriptions differed to some extent, and there were no photographs forthcoming, such as Dr Orbell's, which leave no room for hesitation whatever.'

Prototype of Pukeko

'What is the possibility of a fair-sized colony of the birds existing near Lake Te Anau?'

'It is quite likely that there has been some fluctuations in the numbers of surviving stock, and it may well be that there has been a general increase in the last few years,' said Dr Falla. 'From the reports of conditions in the areas where Dr Orbell found his birds, it would seem that the notornis, like the kiwi, has become well adapted to high country.'

'In what sort of country was the notornis generally supposed to live?'

'In swamps, round shallow tarns and marshy flats.'

'How did the name originate?'

'When specimens such as bones and skeletons crop up, the anatomists used—and still use—a generic or family name from a Greek root. In this way notornis was derived from *ornis* (bird) and *notos* (south).'

'Is there only the one species?'

'Actually there are two closely allied species of the same

genus—one in each Island—but for all practical purposes it is the same bird. But there was another rail, twice as large—the aptornis—and this is known only by its bones. Last summer a party exploring near Waikari, in North Canterbury, found three perfect skeletons of the aptornis in a space of only a few square yards. The notornis is, actually, an old prototype of the common swamp hen or pukeko.'

'Could it be reared in captivity?'

'An experiment would be interesting, but the trouble would be to provide the bird with the nesting and breeding requirements necessary to produce healthy stock. Wild conditions in the isolated country in which it has been found apparently suit it admirably. My opinion is that it is best to leave it where it is, and redouble precautions to prevent vermin such as stray dogs that have gone wild, polecats, stoats, and so on from getting into its habitat. Honorary or official wardens could trap vermin on the borders of the area.'

'What about the element of curiosity in humans?'

'It is natural for anybody going into the Lake Te Anau area to entertain hopes of seeing the notornis; in fact it's become a sort of pilgrimage. But I'm sure that proper protective measures are being taken.'

Value of Sanctuaries

'Does the sanctuary for the Royal Albatross at Taiaroa Head, Otago Harbour, serve its purpose?'

'Certainly; and so also does the sanctuary to the north of Okarito, in South Westland—I won't say exactly where—for white herons, or egrets, and their only known nesting-place in New Zealand.'

'What is the value of a notornis?'

'That's an interesting point. In 1849 W. D. B. Mantell, of Wellington, recognised that there was primarily scientific value in a specimen which he saw sealers at Resolution Island, in Dusky Sound, preparing for the pot. He secured the skin and sent it to the British Museum. The second bird, found by a Maori on Secretary Island, in Thompson Sound in 1851, was also secured by Mantell, and it joined the first in the British Museum. Then in 1878 a rabbiter's dog ran down and captured a live notornis nine miles south-east of the south end of Lake Te Anau. By this time a flourishing trade in natural history rarities had sprung up, and this skin and skeleton were sent to London and later bought by the Dresden Museum for £105. In fact, notornis-hunting became quite a cult.'

There was no further appearance of the elusive notornis till 1898, when J. and D. Ross, camping on the shores of the Middle Fiord, Lake Te Anau, heard a strange bird call. Just before dark, according to the records, one of the brothers' dogs dashed into the bush and reappeared with a bird in its mouth. Sir William Benham (then curator of the Otago Museum) was the first man to dissect the notornis, and he found that this specimen was a healthy young female. The Hon. G. M. Thomson, who examined the stomach contents, was able to confirm the Maori belief that its diet consisted of swamp plants. The bird was bought by the New Zealand government for £250 and placed in the Otago Museum.

Asked to define the attitude of present-day museums when it came to paying for exhibits, Dr Falla said that all reputable museums were quite ready to pay if necessary for specimens which would contribute to knowledge of natural history. But they were just as interested in seeing that species were conserved alive and undisturbed in their own environment. A notornis today might have a certain value among speculators, but as it is absolutely protected, the chances of a speculator disposing of it to a reputable institution were extremely small.

Notornis male in the
snowgrass west of Te Anau.

In earlier days a museum's first thought was to secure the bird; today the main object would be to photograph and study it as far as could be done without molesting it, particularly in the case of such a find as the notornis. 'Naturally,' he added, 'expeditions to the notornis country will go forward with heightened expectations of making useful observations.'

Expedition Next Year

Early next year an expedition sponsored by the New Zealand government will go into the Caswell Sound district to explore the country between that and George Sound, to find out what is happening to the wapiti and red deer. Thirty or more New Zealand scientists and surveyors will be near notornis-inhabited country, and it is possible that they will be able to add something to Dr Orbell's findings. They will be accompanied by an American scientist, Dr Olaus J. Murie, with his son as field assistant. This expedition's principal object will be to investigate the deer population with a view to improving control methods.

. . . this skin and skeleton were sent to London and later bought by the Dresden Museum for £105.

Mainly About Rabbits

by sundowner

21 january 1949

Everyone who travels through Otago and Southland expects to see rabbits. He expects to see them dead on the roads, dead on the fences, and so much alive over the fences that the hillsides seem to have a pulse. That is the expectation and the still popular belief, and there was a time when it bore some relation to the facts.

Today it is just a legend. In a drive of 250 miles through Central and West Otago I may have seen a hundred rabbits altogether—20 or 30 in a creek-bed between Luggate and Lowburn, about as many in the bed of the Manuherikia, and little scampers of twos and threes for about a mile on either side of Raes Junction.

In Southland the situation was a little different. I saw rabbits wherever I saw gorse hedges—especially the old-style hedge with a sod-wall foundation—but three out of four were only a quarter or half grown, and a surprising number were babies sitting quite still at the mouths of burrows. I know that these babies will themselves have babies before winter if they live, and I know that rabbits are not very active in the middle of the day when I did most of my travelling. But I am not blind to the other signs of occupation, and don't have to see the rabbits to know when I am in their country. No one does if rabbits for many years were his only currency—if a pocket-knife meant ten skins, a new tie twenty, a rifle or a visit to town two or three hundred.

I am as little likely to miss the signs of rabbits today as I am to forget the jingles every rabbiter, musterer, shearer, and shed-hand specialised in 50 years ago:

Of rabbits young and rabbits old,
Of rabbits timid and rabbits bold,
Of rabbits tender and rabbits tough,
O thank the Lords we've had enough.

I did however meet a man who told me that he had caught 2000 rabbits last winter on one small block, and another whose tally was 2500. I was assured that £2000 was not an impossible return for a man with a good block, and was supplied with details to prove that one run-holder had made £10,000, less the cost of poison, and the wages and rations of 16 men for eight months at £1 each a day.

But I soon found that rabbit stories were like all hunting stories in this respect—that they varied according to the weather, the mood, and the imagination of the teller; and unlike them in this other respect—that they were 50 per cent political. Whatever is the case in other parts of the Dominion rabbits in Otago and Southland are party politics. If you farm in a Rabbit Board area, rabbits will prevent your right hand from knowing what your left hand is doing. If you are in a free area they will keep you awake at nights wondering what your rates will be when your holding is gathered in too. And whether your representative in parliament is as wise as a serpent or as harmless as a dove he will not escape accusations that he has told one story in Wellington and another over your fence. But if you are so foolish yourself as to seek election to your Board, you

. . . one run-holder had made £10,000, less the cost of poison, and the wages and rations of 16 men for eight months at £1 each a day.

will become a rabbit-farmer, or a netting manipulator, or a trafficker in carrots, or a wink-and-nod man for some purpose other than the speedy and complete destruction of every buck, doe, runner, and sucker above or below ground in your territory.

So at least I gathered by talking first to a free-area farmer, then to a Board-area farmer, then to a rabbiter, then to a farmer-rabbiter, then to a Board member, then to a Board employee. It is true that farmers' troubles are seldom so bad as they sound, but after a few days discussing rabbits from all these different angles, I found myself wondering what had so greatly reduced the rabbit population already, and whether if it is my luck to return to Otago ten years hence I shall see any rabbits at all out of the museum.

I somehow missed it in the newspapers, but was told in Clyde that Parliament had approved of changes in the Rabbit Act that will make rabbits 'as rare as that bird they've just discovered in Southland.'

'Re-discovered,' I said.

'Yes, that's right; found again. The first for 50 years. Well that's how rabbits will be.'

'And what will happen then?'

'The farmers who are crying out now will be down on their knees thanking God. They'll be running ten sheep for every six or seven they run now, and if they stop their burning this country will be what it was when the first settlers saw it.'

'Do you think the tussocks will come back?'

'On the flats—yes. Perhaps not on the rocky faces. But it will be clover and English grasses then, with irrigation in a big way.'

'You're optimistic about the killing?'

'Absolutely. This killer policy will root them right out.'

'Why aren't the farmers rushing it?'

'Because rabbits mean free cash to them. Their wool goes through the firms, but the rabbits are their own.'

'But if they had no rabbits they would not be afraid of the firms. They would have far more sheep.'

'Half as many again. But that doesn't buy a new car or new radio this year. They will of course come to it.'

'You think they will?'

'They will have to under the new Act. But in a year or two they'll be wondering why they ever resisted it.'

'Do many resist?'

'Most farmers resist what is new. If they don't resist it they don't support it. But they're not fools; and when they've had time to think about it they are for it if it is for them.'

'What about the rabbiters?'

'Their day is done—except as wage-earners for the Boards. I'm sorry for them, because their big money has never been easy money. But the country can't afford rabbits, and therefore it can't afford rabbiters or rabbit dealers.'

'There is the existing population of rabbits to dispose of.'

'Not by individuals or firms. The essential point of the new policy is that rabbits will be valueless. It must never again be worthwhile to let a single rabbit live.'

It all sounded convincing to me till I discussed it with a sheep-farmer who had killed his rabbits years ago and wanted to

'But the country can't afford rabbits, and therefore it can't afford rabbiters or rabbit dealers.'

'Rating everybody is like levying a tax on a district every time someone commits theft. Let them catch the thief and collect from him.'

know why he should now be taxed for neighbours who had neglected theirs.

'The Boards have power to put a crippling rate on land—all land—though one man's land may be clear and another's badly infested. But the man who farms his rabbits is an outlaw among his neighbours. They know who he is, and there would be no difficulty in dealing with him. Rating everybody is like levying a tax on a district every time someone commits theft. Let them catch the thief and collect from him.'

'You think rabbit farmers are not very numerous?'

'I'm sure they're not. Farmers hate rabbits. They hate them all the year round. They're as likely to farm them as bee-farmers are to cultivate foul-brood and fruit-farmers to breed codlin moths. Rabbits are vermin to us, and don't forget that they do more than eat grass.'

'I've seen what they can do to young crops.'

I was thinking of trees. Every farmer should plant more trees, and most would if there were no rabbits. But rabbits mean netting fences, so the trees never go in.'

'But you'll now be able to put them in. When the Boards have killed the rabbits the fencing will not be necessary.'

'I'll believe that when I see it. What I've seen so far leaves me with some doubts.'

'Have you seen the bull-dozers at work on the warrens?'

'I've heard that bull-dozers have been used on sandy flats; also rotary hoes. But how far would they get in these gullies?'

'I asked them that question in Central Otago, and the answer was that guns, ferrets, dogs, and cyanide gas would do the job where bull-dozers couldn't be used.'

'That may have been their answer. What I want to see is the dead rabbits.'

'I'm told that you don't see them after the bull-dozers and rotary hoes—that they're smothered in the warrens and stay there.'

'How old are you?'

'Nearly as old as you, I should think.'

'Don't you think we're both old enough not to be bull-dozed ourselves by propaganda? I've seen rabbits come and I've seen them go. They almost disappeared in this district between 1900 and 1910. No one knew why. Now we have to subsidise the districts they like better.'

Auckland After Dark

rosemary vincent
photographer: barbara tipping
6 april 1962

In New Zealand, the coffee bars of Auckland are at present as peculiar to the city as her harbour bridge and cinerama theatre. What distinguishes them from the coffee bars in other centres is their nocturnal activities—not the activities of the patrons, but the actual 'draws' included in the cover charge, the ubiquitous floor-shows that scatter their pleasures among all types and conditions of patrons and are at home anywhere, in dive or loft.

However, the young people who come in evening after evening by bus and car, motor bike, and on foot to places upstairs and downstairs and set back from street level, are not only in search of entertainment. If they were, you wouldn't have the cash-register ringing, the waitress running, the sax wailing and the sandwich-maker concocting as early as they do, well before the floor is billed to be cleared for the show.

They want companionship, these young people: Kiwi companionship which makes you feel one of a crowd, or the bolder sort where you take the initiative and start talking to someone you've never met. And they want atmosphere.

They get both. It's surprising how many friendships are made in a fug of smoke and a jam-packed corner during a twist evening. Atmosphere is nowhere lacking, it depends what point in or around Queen Street you make for, as to what sort you'll get.

One place is pure Parisian, from the two doors marked 'Femmes' and 'Hommes' in one corner to the black back wall with its crazily arrayed, Lautrec-inspired Montmartre people. Caricatures as brassy and shameless as life itself and coloured as loudly—tall hats, long faces, tall hair-dos, long necklines, crooked noses, weirdly curving chins, a grin and a wink, erosion by life around worldly eyes, the French shrug, the universal wickedness. On another wall, by contemporary patterned curtains, a woman washing in a tin basin.

Here, a group called the Mike Walker Trio usually plays in the evening, on a triangle of a stage set in the far corner. Their style is sophisticated and the over-all impression of the place is sophisticated also. Female patrons are noteworthy for the mysterious perfection of their beehive hairstyles. Their escorts, with or without ties, uphold the Ivy League tradition.

Dancers of both sexes are smooth and competent, seldom spectacular; not that the size of the floor and the general feeling are conducive to wildly expressionistic jiving.

But the sophistication is youthfully conscious, and the place is really for the young. Another wall is covered with glossy pin-ups of present and past floor-show entertainers, tall glasses of Coke are served and a roaring trade is done in toasted sandwiches.

Recently a series of Monday-Tuesday twist evenings shattered the Montmartre atmosphere, causing the furniture to be rearranged and attracting into the red shadows jeans and sand-papered shoes, tight skirts and hair-dos rivalling those of the women of Montmartre in height and complexity.

One place is pure Parisian, from the two doors marked 'Femmes' and 'Hommes' in one corner to the black back wall with its crazily arrayed, Lautrec-inspired Montmartre people.

For these evenings five Maori boys made up the band, smiling and clowning as they played, secure behind a curtain of cigarette smoke, a wall of sound and their collective entertainers' name. The problem that waits for the small-town or country boy, arriving in the metropolis with little education and a lot of hope, is no problem here. With something more immediate to think about, these boys were one with each other and with their listeners.

Well, we got a new dance and it goes like this
Bah buppah buppa-buppa-buppa
And the name of the dance is the peppermint twist . . .

The twist has been launched in one of the biggest single campaigns since Elvis Presley's. The manager here, Mr Don Lylian, is glad he cashed in on it, he said—it has paid off. In his opinion the dance is an ingenious gimmick to restore rock 'n' roll to its former position of superiority.

He may be right, only time will tell. But at present it stands on its own—not too energetic (you can do it non-stop for more than 60 hours, others have), not taking up too much floor space, plenty of scope for variation, and having the universal attraction of the hula. Everyone is doing it.

Round and round, up and down,
Round and round and up and down and
One two three kick . . .

And not far away, on the other side of the Town Hall, is another coffee bar where similar sounds rush upstairs to meet you on glad, extrovert waves. The musicians here really know the meaning of team-work, and yet for such a small band they have more than their share of characters.

Heke plays the piano. He is the first person you look for when you come in. Big, squat, impassive until the first real

On noisy nights or during a particularly fetching floor-show this fence shudders with the abortive attempts of long jean-clad legs from outside to clamber over it.

contact of the evening is made between the musicians; and then he looks up and grins, hugely, his face and glasses glinting in the heat and light.

Heke can produce the best of all effects, contentment: you might go through a day that threatens your future as a small crack in a wing threatens an aircraft, but your equilibrium can be restored by seeing Heke. Not only because he is familiar, but because he appears so completely secure in himself, and that sort of feeling is catching.

The bass player and self-styled M.C., Happy, is one of those men with rubber sensibilities. Utterly undisturbed, he cracks jokes through thick and thin and even on off-nights will leave his bass for a moment between items or, still cuddling it, lean across to the mike: 'Have you heard this one . . . ?'

The place is divided into two, the main room and an outdoor coffee garden with striped umbrella within, and tall London-slum houses without, standing up to peer over the corrugated iron fence. On noisy nights or during a particularly fetching floor-show this fence shudders with the abortive attempts of long jean-clad legs from outside to clamber over it. Few try seriously, the kitchen and stage being in full view, but the fence makes a good vantage point if you can hang on for long enough and don't become too excited by the growing frenzy of rhythm from within.

Despite the heat, the main room has to be packed out before the walled-off area under the stars is used. Everyone wants to be near the heart of things. The heart is the band, and the main artery is the wide stone floor sweeping past the stage and curving among tables and wicker chairs to the door, and past the door to the back of the room where couples can practise complicated steps in relative obscurity. Fifty per cent of the inhibitions of fifty per cent of young Aucklanders have been trampled into this stone floor.

Above it is a low ceiling, not too brightly lit, on two walls cubist murals by former Elam Art School teacher Louise Henderson, and another wall of chunky stone that looks like an impression of Byzantine art from a distance.

Everyone here is out to enjoy themselves, and enjoy themselves they will do, no matter how many official helmets are crowding the doorway (particularly on Sunday when the Law says no entertainment allowed). Even when one of those swift, mysterious conferences is seen to take place and the announcement comes that there is to be no floor-show tonight—well, people have still got legs and restless feet. The band's still good for as long as there are people in the room.

Brown skin and white dance together, boy and girl, girl and girl, advertising executive with factory worker, bank clerk with giggling hospital laundress; a sub-editor after late duty tosses off his cares in a frolic between the stage and the kitchen. An elderly man with silvering hair sits among the gyrating hips, attempting expressionlessness. A young couple who have been dancing here for months and know each other's every move kick up their heels in the Charleston, rotate in the twist, leap into rock 'n' roll, hug each other when it works and look bemused when a beat is missed.

There are unexpected shows: the two little teenagers from Wellington, female Elvis Presleys under mountainous hairstyles, the middle-aged Englishman with his tiny ukulele taking us back to the days of bicycles built for two; people filled with Dutch courage by much coffee and twisting, who decide to give it a go and clutch the mike to sing old favourites like 'Who'.

'Shall I sing for you, honey?' a large man wearing tartan carpet slippers asks a girl sitting next to him. He is still slightly inebriated after an earlier party.

'Yes go on, go on!' the girl and half a dozen others urge.

He stands laboriously while the M.C. announces Auckland singer Mr Lofty So-and-So.

'But can you sing?' the girl detains him, suddenly doubtful.

'Don't know yet—soon find out.'

Whether or not he can sing is irrelevant, as long as he chooses a popular number and doesn't outstay his welcome. But if the audience doesn't dig him he should retire gracefully. That is an essential of a coffee bar entertainer—to judge the crowd mood, to know the difference between ovation and slow handclapping, between jeering and cheering, between the sound of feet that stamp in admiration and for less gratifying reasons.

Of course it depends where you are. One coffee bar literally emanates the discreetly smiling attitude of its proprietor that there are to be no extremes here, please: this is no rough-house, gentlemen, this place is respectable.

The manager is a Hungarian who has spent the past four

years in New Zealand and is attempting to smear with a delicate brush some of the Continental atmosphere he remembers on to his establishment, his 'coffee lounge' (a popular word among proprietors).

This one is not Hungary but Paris. The latter still seems to be considered the mecca of romance, night life with a hint of naughtiness; while in general the Kiwi mind sifts from Hungary subjects not really suitable for a gay evening: uprisings, violence, goulash, perhaps.

So there is Paris for the entire length of one wall—the rue by the Seine, the Eiffel Tower, Notre Dame and Montmartre, Paris skies. Paris trees; even the Seine has a Parisian sparkle. On the floor, dozens of little tables and chairs are overshadowed by a multi-coloured carousel, minus the horses. Beneath this glorious object is a full circle of polished wood which belongs to performers at 11 p.m. on Saturday and 1 a.m. on Sunday.

Tables are grouped around it to get the full benefit of singer-comedian Steve Stevenson with his winkle-picker shoes, Cheri with her grass skirt and invisible hula-hoop, Karlo Butocovich giving harmonious voice to one of seven languages, the Duo Revelles (acrobats extraordinaire) and numerous others who come and go.

The Paul Lestre group plays here, with solos by one of their number, John McLaughlin, on piano; or by Paul Lestre himself playing gipsy airs on a violin.

Until recently, music was provided here by the Bob Gillett Orchestra. Bob, a young Californian sax-player trying it out here after his own country and Australia, said there was more to playing in nightclubs or coffee bars by night than simply spinning out a thread of sound for people to chat against. The band was there to entertain. At certain times during the evening they were announced, just as the floor-shows were announced, and the floor was theirs.

So, they hoped, was the attention of the patrons.

'A rumble of conversation isn't always annoying,' Bob said. 'It depends. If people are just talking nonsense—you know—I can feel it's wrong, even if I can't hear what they're saying.'

It was important for everyone, not just musicians but clients as well, to be in the mood. A communal spirit, that's what they strove for.

But the mood did not depend on seeing the participants. Bob said 'When you're in the mood you don't see anything, don't want to.'

Leaving this patch of Paris soil (and coming swiftly down to more familiar earth at the sight of a huhu bug doing its own solitary dance under a street lamp) you walk for a few paces by buildings brooding in their unflourescent loneliness. Then another coffee bar, usually well populated, and if it's not too late you can see the nervous ice-blue flickering of the TV screen on the far wall, and the absorbed backs of heads as the spell settles.

Only the painted figures on the wall are immune, but they are created to be above it anyway—from the welter of dark glasses and matted tresses, tight trousers and open sandals, tired skirts and sagging jerseys, you judge them to be beatniks.

There is a recently established coffee bar in Upper Queen Street looking and feeling its newness, that is intriguing from the street above. You look down a flight of stairs and see a counter with a sign (cover charge 2/6) and you hear pounding of a beat that would make a newly civilised African tribesman have second thoughts.

At the bottom of the stairs you see a ceiling decoration of short red stalactites, a wall mirror here, potted plants there, plushness everywhere. Travel posters in one corner expound the glories of Rangoon and Saigon. The musicians sweat it out

Throughout the evening there is a steady decrease in tension, and inhibitions, a steady increase in awareness of the stuff of life.

The floor is not big enough now for the crowd that has gathered. The floors are never big enough when the vague thought of dancing has become a compulsion. Either the place is so empty that you dare not, or else it is so crowded that the mere swing of an elbow could cause concussion. Throughout the evening there is a steady decrease in tension, and inhibitions, a steady increase in awareness of the stuff of life.

If the coffee bar's peak hour could be arrested in time and then stretched to eternity, psychiatrists would be out of business. But it has to end every night, not with a bang but a yawn; a stubbing of the last cigarette, a fumbling for coats, a climb upstairs, a smile at the baggy-eyed proprietor leaning over his counter wondering who and how and why; with a hailing of taxis, a whirring of motor bikes or a deep breath (fresh air) before the long trek home on twist-tired feet.

One o'clock, two o'clock, three o'clock: the reprimanding dial on the Town Hall tower is sole witness to the drifting generation's mass dispersal.

in shirt-sleeves and a pretty girl in a dress that is sack to the waist and then fish-tail stands in round-eyed sincerity before the mike.

One wall is covered with large beer-barrel corks in parallel lines, an impression of the latest in modern architecture. This is presumably an Islanders' paradise, for people of dark skin and peaceful countenance are everywhere, dancing and sitting, living and watching others live.

For every three beautiful Island girls with serene faces and sensuous hips, for every three young men languidly on the look-out there is at least one large Island mama sitting at a table in calm contemplation. One, although short, is encased in rolls of fat that speak of a supremely contented existence. Another of more normal proportions, iron-haired, sits upright with a slight proud smile that turns into a beam when she sights a friend across the room.

Against this happy drift from the south there is the irresistible force of the poor white, the big guy with his crisp new notes and his vivid past, the doll with straw beehive and a divine vacuum of a face.

Isle of the
Setting Sun

18 november 1966

In the Town Hall at Halfmoon Bay, there hangs a picture of King George V. Recently, so the story goes, a visitor went into the hall, saw the picture and said, 'I've got news for you. He's dead.' This story, although probably apocryphal, illustrates the leisurely way of life on Stewart Island.

The whole economy of the island and its 540 inhabitants is based on the fishing industry, and a large fleet of boats operates from Halfmoon Bay. The boats go after fish, and oysters from the Foveaux Strait beds, and muttonbirds are taken from the islands off the coast.

The important part fishing plays in the everyday lives of almost everybody on the island can be gauged from the columns of the *Rakiura Herald*, the island's only newspaper produced by the schoolchildren. A large number of the items and stories in it are directly connected with fishing, and a 'Shipping News' column gives snippets of information on the activities of the fishing fleet.

Community spirit is very strong on Stewart Island— everybody knows everybody else, and there is always a helping hand where and when needed. The influence of television has been felt even in this remote area, however, with the result that some activities, such as the 'local pictures', which now function only during the height of the tourist season, have been forced to close down because of lack of support. Even so, celebrations such as 21st birthday parties are thrown open to the whole of the island simply by placing an announcement on the notice board at Halfmoon Bay.

The link with the South Island, or 'The Mainland' as the islanders call it, is the Government ferry *Wairua* which runs between Bluff and Halfmoon Bay—a distance of about 20 miles. From a distance, Halfmoon Bay looks very attractive with boats bobbing at anchor, the broad sweep of the beach, and the houses nestled in the trees. Closer in, it becomes apparent that the beach, like many beaches, could be cleaner, and that the township itself looks untidy with untrimmed grass verges. Rates are low, however, and the council is stretched to its limit maintaining the 12 miles of formed road on the island. Even if there were sufficient money for improvements in the township, it would be difficult to decide where to start.

Many transactions are carried out by the barter system in this leisurely corner of New Zealand. One man who owns the only quarry on the island recently asked—and got—three yards of crushed metal in payment for rock supplied to the council.

There is a small tourist industry, but it is not flourishing. Islanders in the main are indifferent to tourists—they don't mind their presence, but they do not encourage it. As one man said, 'When they're all over here, you have trouble getting up to the bar in the pub.'

Most tourists who visit the island expect to be able to walk around it in an hour, and are surprised when they find out how large it is—670 square miles.

The first European to sight Stewart Island was Captain James Cook during his search for a southern continent in 1770. At first he thought it was an island, but later changed his mind, and decided that what he had seen was a peninsula jutting out from the South Island. As such it appears on his first map of New Zealand, under the name South Cape.

Cook sailed round the island, but did not at any stage land. The honour of being the first European to land probably belongs to Captain Oliphant of the sealer *Endeavour*, who was collecting skins in the area during 1803.

Foveaux Strait, separating the island from the South Island, was first discovered in 1806 by an American sealer, O. F. Smith, who was commanding a vessel named the

Halfmoon Bay from Moturau Moana.

Following his investigations, a price of £6000 was offered and, after some negotiation, accepted by the Maoris on June 29, 1864.

Favourite. Although he had previously been refused permission to land at Sydney while commanding another vessel, Smith apparently felt no animosity, for he named the strait after Major Joseph Foveaux, aide to Governor King, of New South Wales.

In 1809 the ship *Pegasus* under the command of Captain S. Chase sailed to the island. Her first officer was a William Stewart, who undertook a detailed survey of the area now known as Port Pegasus. In doing so he gave his name to the island as the first person to undertake any detailed survey work on it. For the next few years Stewart's Island was visited by whalers and sealers, some of whom set up camps. A few of these camps were raided by Maoris, and the inhabitants eaten.

Sixteen years after his first visit, Stewart returned to Port Pegasus to found a trading settlement, dealing mainly in timber and flax. The next year he built a ship and timber yard, but both these ventures collapsed, and Stewart spent some time in prison in Sydney for debt.

Shortly after this, a colony of whalers who had married Maori women set themselves up on Codfish Island, off the coast. The first permanent settlement on Stewart Island was made by a mixture of renegade whalers, ship deserters and

Maoris at Paterson Inlet, into which flow the island's two main streams.

In 1840 the Treaty of Waitangi, giving the Crown sovereign rights over New Zealand, was signed, and Captain J. Nias, commander of HMS *Herald*, was ordered to take Major Thomas Bunbury of the 80th Regiment to the island to collect the signatures of the local Maori chiefs.

As pilot he took William Stewart, who by this time had returned to the country, and had offered his services without payment. Although the signatures were collected satisfactorily, the island still belonged to the Maoris. At first, Superintendent John McAndrew of the province of Otago wanted to buy it, but when Southland formed a separate provincial government, the plan was hastily abandoned.

In 1860 Chief Topi Patuki, also known as John Topi, wrote to Governor Gore-Brown, offering the island for sale. Nothing was done about the offer until 1863, when a Mr Heale, under directions from the Fox-Whitaker coalition government, sailed around the island to assess its value. Following his investigations, a price of £6000 was offered and, after some negotiation, accepted by the Maoris on June 29, 1864.

Although known to Europeans by the somewhat prosaic name of Stewart Island, the island was originally called by the Maoris Te Puke a te Waka a Maui (The Anchor-stone of Maui's Canoe). This, however, was more of an honorific title, and the popular Maori name was Rakiura or Island of the Setting Sun.

Oban, Halfmoon Bay.

The Mount:
Beautiful
and Booming

conon fraser

10 january 1972

One's first impression of Mount Maunganui is that it is vigorous and booming. Inclined to sprawl, it obviously has plenty of room to do so. A large proportion of the business, administrative and municipal buildings are new and of pleasing architectural design, and the industrial area of fertiliser works, grain mills, oil storage tanks and warehouses near the port is well organised and highly efficient. The port itself has the fastest cargo handling facilities in the country and serves the Bay of Plenty and the man-made forests of the Volcanic Plateau. It has the country's third greatest turnover in tonnage and is our leading export port, handling mainly wood pulp, newsprint, sawn timber, logs, milk products and butter. Its deep-water wharf invariably has an impressive line up of ships, a large proportion of them from Japan, and further reclamation and wharf extensions are under way on both the Mount and Tauranga sides of the harbour. It is chiefly this virile and expanding economy which has given the district the fastest population growth rate in New Zealand.

It is remarkable that such a port, handling 2½ million tons a year, should also be one of our major and most progressive holiday resorts. Napier has its port and esplanade, but the port is tucked round the corner at West Shore, whereas at the Mount the wharves and the harbour beach, enjoyed by thousands every summer, successfully co-exist alongside one another—the dividing line between toil and leisure being no more than the wooden jetty of the cross-harbour ferry. The beach is clean and safe for bathing, and the wharves and overseas ships are in fact a popular holiday attraction.

Perhaps, because of the speed at which it has grown, it is difficult to realise that Mount Maunganui is still basically a small town. Tauranga has been larger for longer and has a steadier population, with a considerable number of retired people who have chosen it for its mild and sunny climate. But

the Mount has the disadvantage—to its ratepayers certainly—of a population of 8500 that leaps to 30–40,000 over Christmas and New Year, with an additional 20,000 day-trippers on summer weekends. With good road and rail communications and an airport it is easy to reach, especially from Auckland, Hamilton, the Waikato, Rotorua, and other parts of the Bay of Plenty. 'Regulars' include Waikato farmers during the season, and the proportion of South Island visitors, while still insignificant, increases during the winter.

The number of overseas tourists who visit the Mount is negligible. Its appeal is to families and young people looking for somewhere that is lively and not too sophisticated—in fact a free and easy place with a wide choice of things to do.

Mount Maunganui has plenty to offer for this sort of holiday: the sheltered harbour beach is perfect for small children and elderly people who prefer the shade to the sun; there is a magnificent surfing beach only a few hundred yards across the peninsula, and surfcasting and solitude along a shore backed by dunes that reaches south for miles down the Bay of Plenty coast. Moturiki Island, which more or less divides the popular ocean beach from the lonelier one, has a 'blowhole' through which the surf booms in rough weather, and is linked to the shore by a sand causeway. At the head of the peninsula is 'The Mount' itself, 762 feet high, with extensive views of the port and town below, of Tauranga harbour and the ranges inland, and Matakana Island across the narrow harbour entrance, covered in pine plantations and carrying on the long sweep of the Bay of Plenty north. A walking track round the base of the hill, shaded by pohutukawas, leads to rock pools and quiet fishing spots.

It is hardly surprising that development of some of these natural features as 'tourist attractions' should have caused controversy in the past. Many felt that the Mount itself, as a particularly striking landmark, should have been left alone, not only because it is an ancient pa site, but because of its personification in Maori legend and the regard which many Maoris still have for it. But it has been steadily encroached upon. Much of the bush on its slopes has been cleared and in the last three years or so a road has been carved to take tourists to the summit by four-wheel drive vehicle during the summer. The next proposal and one that seems inevitable, is for a cable car to the summit, which would bring in much-needed revenue and give a greater number of people the chance to enjoy a view that had to be won before.

Less controversial, but by no means easy, has been the establishment of Marineland on Moturiki Island by a company which bought the rights of the old quarry there in 1966 and blasted the present six pools, which contain half a million gallons of seawater, out of solid rock. Its natural setting gives this 'seaquarium' an advantage over Napier's Marineland, and it is reputed to have the largest collection of marine mammals in the Southern Hemisphere.

Other tourist attractions which have marked Mount Maunganui's growth are the Bay Park raceway, a third golf course which is taking shape near the aerodrome, and a natural hot salt water pool which is claimed to be beneficial to people suffering from arthritis and lumbago and the only one of its sort in the world. Peter Sorrenson, owner of Marineland, hopes to tap a similar reservoir of heated water from a depth of 3–400 feet for a tropical aquarium. This may not be possible for several years and is likely to be costly, but he is determined that what he does eventually have will be unequalled anywhere.

Tauranga's big game fishing off Mayor Island has been famous for years. Unfortunately, catches have fallen drastically—some blame the Japanese fishing fleets—but local experts optimistically claim that with up to date techniques being used a level has been reached and the incentive is as strong as ever. There is, anyway, some compensation in the fact that the water around Mayor Island is some of the clearest in the country for skindiving and spearfishing.

The Mount has not developed as a popular tourist resort without some sacrifices. George Capper, president of its Jaycees, considers that the biggest has been its change from a comparatively quiet and restful seaside town to one that is perhaps all out to attract more holidaymakers. Yet even if these people come only for the day, they expect to find boat launching ramps, adequate toilet facilities and a clean and well-kept town. The burden of providing these falls on the borough council and ratepayers, and other projects of equal urgency to residents have had to be shelved. I noticed, for example, that many streets are poorly lit at night. Sewage is an urgent problem, as Mount Maunganui uses septic tanks and still has no treatment plant. The exact details of a scheme estimated at £600,000 in 1959, debated or delayed ever since and now likely to cost nearer $4 million, have not yet been decided on. But the danger of pollution to the harbour increases each year, and this is certainly recognised.

There is also a growing need for better communication

The next proposal and one that seems inevitable, is for a cable car to the summit, which would bring in much-needed revenue . . .

The first impression of vigour is strengthened by a confident policy that everyone should pull together to make the place swing

between the boroughs of Tauranga and Mount Manuganui. Visitors are often surprised to find two quite distinct places separated not only by 12 miles of road but conflicting interests as well. It has been pointed out that a bridge across the harbour would cut the distance between the boroughs to $3\frac{1}{2}$ miles and help to bridge differences as well. The airport, at the Mount, would effectively be brought nine miles closer to Tauranga, and unity be given to the port facilities being developed on both sides of the harbour. Transport would be cheaper, and this will become increasingly important with the completion of the Kaimai tunnel. Tourists to both places would be able to make and alter plans more easily. The benefits are obvious, but the cost would be tremendous. The issues of where to build the bridge and to what design have been debated for years although not always with asperity; at a packed meeting in the Tauranga town hall last year, it is reported that 'the audience was in a fine humour throughout the meeting and at times the remarks from both the panel and the floor were so amusing that people laughed until tears came to their eyes'.

Another of Mount Maunganui's immediate problems is that of coping with its exceptional summer influx. Shops and restaurants have come a long way, and there are now a large number of burger bars and fish and chip shops, which are what holidaymakers want. The number of motor camps, camping grounds and especially motel accommodation have all increased tremendously in the past ten years, although the hotel situation has actually deteriorated. The Mount has no private hotels, while Tauranga, with 13 in 1958, now has only four. The changing pattern of holidaymaking is reflected in this decline and in the increased use of motels. The first motel was opened at Tauranga in 1953. By 1963 the Mount had three motels and today has 15, while Tauranga has 26. Motels these days tend to be larger, and in fact the number of motel beds at the Mount have gone up by 856 per cent in the last 10 years, to cope with the relatively short season.

The first impression of vigour is strengthened by a confident policy that everyone should pull together to make the place swing, especially with first class entertainment and diversions over Christmas and New Year to combat the threat of insurgent hooliganism that created such chaos in 1969. There is a determination that the Mount should not only hold its leading place as a major resort, but expand and make even more of its assets and beautiful location. Tauranga, quieter and full of history, balances a slightly brash but popular partner that knows what it wants, and is confident that nothing is likely to stop it.

Pride of the Avon

bruce mason

photographer: roy sinclair

23 october 1972

'To lose one Town Hall, Sir, may be regarded as a misfortune; to lose two, looks like carelessness', to adapt Lady Bracknell's reproof to John Worthing on his lack of parents. Wonderful and providential carelessness! For both Christchurch Town Halls, the modest first of timber, its bulkier neighbour of stone, were wrecked by earthquake and fire more than a century ago.

What now presides majestically over the Avon would not have been possible without nature's benign cataclysm, and the careless hand that lit the match or dropped the butt or overturned the paraffin lamp.

Auckland, Wellington and Dunedin are saddled with and stuck with, to Kingdom come or earthquake, intimidating grey piles of Birmingham Gothic, exact images in stone of Victorian bigwiggery and smugness, ranging their citizens within as in a schoolroom, sitting them below a high stage on which their masters strut and fret like surrogate parents.

In Christchurch, we are ushered into a friendly, acoustic space, ranged above and all around a central point. The grandeur of the building, its grace and benign accommodation to civic needs, rather than as bolster to civic pride (though this, too), have launched Christchurch in a blow and with a flash (trumpet fanfare off, by John Ritchie) as New Zealand's premier city.

I couldn't doubt this, walking over the building, and taking in Christchurch itself as backdrop and ground—'clad in its glorious spring regalia'—His Worship, Mr Pickering, in justifiably lush vein—sighting the Town Hall from every angle and vantage point, admiring the skill of the architects (Warren and Mahoney) for offering the eye so various a vista, enticing from every station. The plan of the building, reproduced in all the handsome programmes, suggests, according to your persuasion, a beetle, or a nuclear rocket, and you can choose either image and find it appropriate.

If a beetle, then its head is the 1008-seat James Hay Theatre, its body and trunk the enormous foyer, its 22,000 square feet of Carrara marble, the explosions of light and glass and its acres of red and polished timber, with a duct leading to The Limes Restaurant, and the spreading tail is the great auditorium itself, holding 2662, provision for a choir of 400 and an orchestra of 100.

If a rocket, then see it zooming into the heart and mind of every citizen of Christchurch.

If your image is zoological, dismiss from your mind any possible suggestion that this will be a white elephant: the Town Hall is now the focus and centre of the city, displacing at last Cathedral Square, which forfeited its place years ago to commercial barbarities and—more recently—to the lowering great heaps of the Ministry of Works, dwarfing its scale and menacing its proportions.

I took a little time to accommodate to the murals of Patrick Hanly, which encircle the conference room on the first floor vestibule: a frieze of coloured fingers, red and green the major colours, but later viewings convinced me that they were exactly right, breaking up the solemnities, and beautifully undercutting what might, without them, have been a 'palace of culture' heaviness. Everywhere the building has been called a 'complex', partly to indicate the future buildings which will later join it, but might I beseech everyone, from His Excellency down, that a more graceful word would serve better? A complex could be any old pile or heap or collection; let's have a competition for a neater name. First entry, though unlikely to win the prize: structures.

The official opening on Saturday, September 30, was solemn without stuffiness, with two distinguished presences, Sir Denis Blundell, and Mr W. H. Hayes, Lord Mayor of Adelaide, speaking agreeably and easily, and His Excellency is a fast man for a homely quip. Mr Pickering, presiding, showed a light and pretty wit. All the bodies involved in the building were represented, and the speeches invited one to feel the powerful communal grip of Christchurch on its citizens, without which a city is only a collection of people living cheek by jowl.

To this communal spirit they owe, one cannot doubt, the finest Town Hall of its size in the world. John Ritchie composed, and the Skellerup Woolston Band ringingly delivered some invigorating fanfares and flourishes, the Cathedral Choristers, a squad of red lozenges, sang like angels, the Christchurch Liedertafel sang songs by Vernon Griffiths and Sibelius, reminding one of how prodigally endowed this city is with fine choirs. The opening ended with a Vice-Regal touch to the plunger which would start the fountain in that part of the Avon which now washes the walls of the Town Hall on the Victoria Square aspect—it was sluggish for a few minutes, and some of us collected round a hole leading to intricate electric bowels where anxious men tinkered—but a few moments later, three gigantic water-puff balls played.

The Inaugural Concert in the evening was a splendid occasion, with every one of the 2662 seats occupied, and the entire choir area filled by the ladies and gentlemen of the Royal Christchurch Musical Society, and the Christchurch Harmonic Society (get those names right, or choral wrath will be terrible!), with the Royal ladies flanking the area, in dresses suggesting vestal virgins ripe for ritual immersion, the Harmonic ladies at the rear, as a hunting-green collar for the sober dinner suits of the men. Awesome moment when both choirs stood up: it was like a huge bed of flowers bursting into bloom.

The programme was designed from celebratory rather

. . . with the Royal ladies flanking the area, in dresses suggesting vestal virgins ripe for ritual immersion

than musical criteria, and no breath of criticism from me for this. A smartly liveried Canterbury Representative Band brilliantly showed their skill in another John Ritchie flourish, in *Prelude for an Occasion*, by E. Gregson, and in Bliss's *Kenilworth Suite*, written as the test piece for the Crystal Palace competition in 1936, and the band also played for *A Christchurch Cantata* by the British composer Eric Ball. Mr Field-Dodgson coaxed from choir and band a luminous performance of a most winning work, agreeably scored for brass, and offering the choir a wide range of sonorities. Pious without a hint of stodginess, it proved ideal for the occasion.

After a lengthy interval, in which the audience was invited to inspect the pleasances and amenities, John Ritchie conducted the Christchurch Civic Orchestra in a performance of the Beethoven Fifth Symphony which, if it did not achieve grandeur, had much fine playing in the quieter episodes, notably in the second movement, and to the finale, Beethoven's little-performed Fantasia in C minor for piano chorus and orchestra, which happily combined the talents and energies of the Christchurch Harmonic Society, the Civic Orchestra and Maurice Till. Much of the piano writing is like an extended Beethoven cadenza, and Mr Till gave it an immaculate polish, and demonstrated the splendid tone and

The three gigantic water puff-balls of the Town Hall fountain.

range of the new Steinway; the choral section is like an early work-out for the *Hymn to Joy*, and the piece proved entirely fitting for what its selectors wanted.

The acoustics of the auditorium, much laboured over by Dr Marshall from the University of Western Australia, are admirable and even astonishing; someone 20 rows away from me had the temerity to open a sweet during the Cantata: I hope it never reached its destination. Its wrapping crackled like the air-mail edition of the London *Times* and the noise was soon extinguished by outraged hisses.

The James Hay Theatre was off-limits until Sunday; rumour talked of Dame Ngaio up all night for a week on end. She had had trouble getting lights, and what we saw for her production of *Henry V* were assembled from all over Christchurch. The theatre has a handsome, timbered richness; the 1308 seats are arranged so that the effect is one of proximity to the stage from every part of the house and of a most accommodating and welcoming intimacy.

The opening to the play was dazzling and unforgettable: the curtain rose to snow swirling blue mists (of time, I took it) from which Jonathan Elsom, as Chorus dressed as the Droushoet portrait of Shakespeare and astoundingly life like, emerged to speak to us the lines which Dame Ngaio suggests to us Shakespeare may have written for himself. It was a brilliant notion, which Dame Ngaio, in the programme note invited us 'to entertain and humour', and Mr Elsom's performance, a masterpiece of elegance, clarity and style allowed us even more than this.

The play marched along briskly and urgently, offering a fine Henry, tough and somewhat bewildered by the fate thrust on him, in David Hindin (who is alternating the part with Desmond Woods), a splendid Mistress Quickly in Mildred Wood—her scene on the death of Falstaff was one of the

Its wrapping crackled like the air-mail edition of the London *Times* and the noise was soon extinguished by outraged hisses.

triumphs of the night—and a dozen or so other very capable and ringing performances. Dame Ngaio achieved heraldic simplicity in the second half, and that despatch and swiftness of attack that has always marked her work: She appeared at the end, the most sumptuous of blue birds, to receive the unmistakable homage of her city.

So that was Christchurch's party:
In Xanadu did Kubla Khan,
A stately pleasure dome decree

The decree worked in Christchurch too. We have something here of the boldest imagination, with nothing skimped or scamped or botched. I hold it to be an augury, a sign of emboldening times. It does not surprise me at all that this should have happened in Christchurch.

The Building of a Beehive

alan thorley

photographer:
bill beavis

18 october 1975

Whoever first attempted to equate New Zealand with the Biblical 'land of milk and honey' might agree the comparison doesn't stand up too well in today's age of inflating costs and overseas borrowing.

But critics of the expense and lavishness of design that is going into the Parliament building additions might, with a little imagination, see a more odious comparison. The taxpayer is the one being milked to finance the building of the Beehive, from which the drones can be counted on to produce their election honey.

'The Beehive' is one of the gentler descriptions conferred on the giant blancmange which, from as early as next September, will begin taking over most of parliament's administrative and social functions.

The controversial design, conceived by the British architect Sir Basil Spence and developed by New Zealand government architects, has been variously described as 'an imperial echo which filtered through the mind of a bored architect', a pyramid of poor taste, and some choicer names which would send even the most bumbling bee crimson.

'There it will sit,' complained MP Eddie Isbey in 1971, 'sticking out like a sore thumb against an alien environment like some monstrous, expensive joke.'

Expensive yes, but fears that the Beehive might, like the Sydney Opera House, become a victim of spiralling costs look to be unfounded. A joke? Some detractors might still maintain so, but as the Beehive gradually takes shape, concrete-and-steel cell by concrete-and-steel cell, the criticism is quietening.

'Now that the scaffolding has gone,' noted the *New Zealand Herald* recently, 'Wellingtonians and those from outside who visit the capital find the growing structure increasingly pleasing.' In a country all too lacking in public buildings of architectural originality, said the *Herald*, the

'The Beehive' is one of the gentler descriptions conferred on the giant blancmange

Beehive was emerging as a distinctive and unique centrepiece for a cluster of new state buildings.

The capital's motherly *Evening Post*, at last with an offspring that Wellington could compare to Christchurch's town hall or the Auckland harbour bridge, clucked proudly that the Beehive was 'a handsome addition to Parliament and a change from the conventional glass and steel structure' (it is, of course, an *unconventional* glass and steel structure).

'I think,' adds Sid Bates, the Ministry of Works design architect for the Beehive project, 'that you're either going to think it's very good or very bad. And, frankly, I'd rather take the chance than have a building that was just mediocre.'

One of the most important requirements of the Beehive was that it must blend in with the existing Parliament buildings, adopting the same rhythm, scale, and balance of light and shade. External facing materials will also look singular: a granite facing for the podium, or solid rectangular base, and the upper portions of the Beehive in marble veneer where appropriate

But there's an inherent irony in the news that the old parliament buildings are now considered an earthquake risk. Almost overnight, the Beehive has become the focal point around which the rest of parliament will have to be designed. Anticipating the demolition of Parliament House, the Beehive architects have abandoned their original intention of linking the two buildings by bridges at the first, second and third floors.

The beginnings of the Beehive.

Now there will be a link only at the first floor.

Meanwhile, the once-serene grounds of Parliament abuzz with workers, the Beehive grows inexorably upward, its easy curves providing relief from a jagged city skyline. Work is well up to schedule: in early September, workmen were pouring concrete on the 8th floor.

The lower floors are being finished in tawa panelling, marble facings, and bronze aluminium to match the window frames encircling honey-coloured glass. A rustic carpet (with a circular pattern, naturally) has been chosen; and Ministry of Works and Development designers are preparing a submission on interior furnishings.

The visitor to the Beehive will have a choice of entry. If he comes in by the basement pedestrian access from Bowen St he will pass by the business end of things: huge air-conditioning ducts, twin emergency diesel generators, the PABX system, car ramps, a cooling tower (which in a normal building would be on the roof)—even the Beehive's own transformer substation.

In the core of the Beehive will be a series of public lifts, one specially for MPs, and—hidden away behind a door which can be opened with only the one pass-key—a lift for the exclusive use of the Prime Minister.

The more usual entry for visitors and VIPs will be either from Parliament House on the first floor or by the ground-floor main entrance on the north flank of the podium. This leads into a spacious tawa-panelled foyer, to the right of which is a television/radio studio (to keep Ministers from having to flit to Avalon or elsewhere) and a lecture room/theatre seating 150 people. To the left, public cloakrooms, a staff cafeteria, and the main kitchens from which food will be delivered by service hoists to upwards of 500 people in the dining and function rooms above.

But the invited guest would see none of this. He will be enticed by the Guy Ngan-Joan Calvert tapestry wall-hanging direct from the main entrance up a wide grand stair flanked by marble to the first floor, around the circular pillar hiding a VIP toilet, then into the main reception room—the full height of the drum—looking out over Wellington harbour.

Here is where John Drawbridge's winning mural (now in storage on site) will be hung along the curving inner wall, leading in at the far or southern end to a member's dining room and, on the mezzanine-like second floor above, the member's bar.

The second and third floors are littered with bars, dining rooms and lounges, sufficient to paralyse the unaccustomed drone far quicker and more effectively than an entire stock of supermarket fly spray.

But the Beehive isn't all pleasure. Above the circular drum will rise the floors of ministerial offices, each floor reducing in diameter, surmounted by the Prime Minister's suite and Cabinet room floors—and, finally, a viewing deck.

The timber panelling will also undergo subtle variations, from rimu for the ministerial floors to mangeao for the 8th and 9th to kohekohe (botanically a true mahogany) on the viewing deck.

The Beehive has actually already been used. The National Film Unit requested, and was granted, permission to show *This is New Zealand* to a judiciary conference in the ground-floor theatre.

But the shift proper will begin around next September when Bellamy's moves in, allowing for demolition of the old wartime timber-hutted extensions to make way for a car park. The likely date for full occupation is early 1978, depending on the weather and variables in the building industry. At that stage, the last of the workers will leave, and the drones will

The second and third floors are littered with bars, dining rooms and lounges, sufficient to paralyse the unaccustomed drone far quicker and more effectively than an entire stock of supermarket fly spray.

occupy the beehive *en masse*. Depending on the solemnlty accorded the opening, there might even be a Queen.

The occupancy of the Beehive probably won't change much. The odd drone may come and go every three years or so; most, however, can count on a fairly long residency. But of course everyone knows what happens to a drone when he loses his sting. He goes to a nicer world, higher in the sky. It's on the 10th floor and they call it Cabinet.

A Litter of
Students

WEIR HOUSE

1932

1ᴬ

susan woodhouse
photographer: peter bush
20 december 1975

Our garden is full of darts and toilet paper. It is because we live beneath Weir House, a university hostel for male students. About once a day the students lean from the Georgian windows and throw loo paper and darts with logarithms on them, or bruised fruit and fireworks in season.

The suburb of Kelburn in Wellington is geographically shaped to their advantage. They live up in the circle. We live, like sitting ducks, in the stalls. A really brisk Wellington wind will carry their missiles to the stage, the IBM building on The Terrace.

University final exams were in November but that didn't reduce the ejections from Weir House. The students celebrated Guy Fawkes, every night for two weeks, with rocket launchings from the hostel to the harbour. Then for breakfast each morning they exploded Tom Thumbs in peace shattering packet-loads.

These, plus the sight of our sycamore trees strangling in Purex and the occasional broken beer bottle jutting from the weeds, made me feel middle-aged and anti-students; against my wishes because I remember being a student nine years ago. But they were forcing me into it.

The 'Them and Us' demarcation between the students and public is partly due to the way students preach anti-conformism as soon as they hit university and then set about conforming like mad to a 'student' image. The public thinks it is smug and silly. The students think of it as a survival kit in a world full of institutions and generation gaps.

Are the students who litter Kelburn from their hostel windows conforming to the image of the hard working student who needs relief, maybe. I asked a girlfriend to come with me to Weir House to find out about the psychology of chucking stuff out of windows.

We went straight to the top storey from which the bulk of material is thrown. We chose a door, knocked and a couple of Asian students opened up.

'Hello. We are doing a survey on projectiles. Have you anything to say about them?'

They seemed confused. Julie explained that we were looking for throwers and that they didn't look like throwers but perhaps they could recommend some.

'Ah, yes, I think' said one who burst into understanding with a wild grin. 'You need rooms 14 and 15.'

Our thanks were drowned by a snap of gunpowder ten yards down the corridor.

The next door was opened by Kiwi boys, hairy, pale and suspicious. We told them about our projectiles survey and asked if we could come in and talk.

'You two anthropology students?' asked a tall thin boy with afro curls and rimless spectacles.

'No. We are simply interested in what and why people throw. For example, do certain targets excite you?'

A student with a beard but no moustache, who looked kind of nude under the nose, said targets were extremely important. Everton Hall, a student hostel below Weir House, was a prime target. Especially during the Guy Fawkes season. Some highly successful raids were executed by planting

Weir House looks out over The Terrace to the harbour beyond.

'We are simply interested in what and why people throw. For example, do certain targets excite you?'

powerful fireworks outside the hostel at midnight.

Exams were in progress. However it was believed that the midnight blasts would stir the students up and make them alert for the morrow's test.

The cable car was another good target because it moved. With 20 pieces of fruit the chances are you would only hit the cable car once. A successful hit was as good as having sex, a student told us. He explained that a bitter disappointment in his life was a thwarted raid on the cable car when it carried former president Lyndon Johnson and Ladybird up to Kelburn. There were security guards at every cable car window and not one of the massive supply of flour bags and apples was thrown.

Private houses were not intentional targets. But you could not always gauge a wind, you follow? Capricious gusts blew missiles kilometres off course. Just the other day an unusual wind carried a roll of toilet paper up behind Weir House. It came to rest, bedraggled and unravelled, around a proud tree in the garden of the Japanese embassy.

'Some things are definitely better to throw than others,' said one of the students. 'Obscenities are vivid projectiles. Toilet paper's okay. Covers a large area. You will have to ask Tiscot about that. He's ex-champion. He got a roll as far as Taranaki Street once. It wrapped itself round the spire of the Greek Orthodox church.'

'Darts are good. Fruit. It's a tradition in Weir House to see someone and throw an apple at him. We throw only biodegradable things. Beer bottles? Whoever threw those must have been drunk.'

Julie and I asked Luccio Casagrander (Luke Bighouse in English) who is a chef at Weir House, about the fruit. He said that the students would grow to be strong and sound if they put more of it into their stomachs and less out their bedroom windows. The fruits most popular with the students were those with the highest squashing potential. Apples and pears were undoubtedly good sloshers.

The most famous projectile of all, according to a science student with a pale face and a maniacal grin, was the sky-rocket. He dashed out of the room and returned with a sawn-off vacuum cleaner pipe which he stroked affectionately.

'You block up one end and it becomes a rocket launcher. Insert the stick end of the rocket in the pipe. Light up and launch. You get amazing range and accuracy with this device.'

He reached over to his desk and showed us a couple of pages of equations which he had worked out to assist him with the launchings.

'This is really a child's game and you are almost an adult. Do children look down on you with scorn?'

'No. I am taller than they are. You see, there is great joy in throwing. It's futile but basically stirring. There is pleasure in seeing something flying toward its target.'

'Does living high up encourage one to throw?'

'Indeed. We feel we are in a medieval castle fighting and defending on the ramparts. C Floor has a good balcony.'

'But don't the Asian students make you feel ashamed with their restraint?'

'Don't you read the newspapers? They thrive on anonymity.'

'Do you throw in order to become well known?'

'I don't write my name on my rockets. There is a $10 fine for throwing.'

A student who was leaning on a biscuit tin with a leopard-skin pattern suddenly cut in.

'Look, who is your lecturer? Who asked you to do this survey?'

'You treat us like Muslim women. We are not chaperoned

The fruits most popular with the students were those with the highest squashing potential.

by our husbands, brothers or uncles. We have come on our own account,' said Julie.

'Okay. Well, on behalf of us, I say if you have got something to throw then throw it. People have been throwing things through the ages.'

We say thanks and go off to find Tiscot, the ex-loo-roll-chucking champion. When we found him he was studying for his law exams but he was friendly and didn't mind sparing us a minute for our survey. He made one thing clear at the outset. Toilet paper was not a base missile. You didn't throw it. You flew it. In Tiscot's view, loo roll flying was an art form.

'One roll is approximately 50 feet long. A vigorous wind will do it justice. The paper will whirl and twirl.'

'And furl,' I said. 'Around private property.'

'Pure error. We were not interested in small-fry targets. Returning to winds, a strong one will rip the paper. You learn to judge which are best. The method is simple. Hold a stick through the roll loosely enough to let it unwind. Practise in winter. Summer foliage blocks the way.'

Tiscot said that during his year at Weir House there was a phenomenal consumption of toilet paper per capita. Once, three floors were out of it. Tiscot gave up his art form when the warden threatened to introduce Jeyes.

All Life is There

kit frost

photographer: robin morrison

may 1977

HALLELUJAH! The country is alive and well and living not far from the ever-so-civilised city. There we were, urbane city folk condescending to spend a day at an A and P Show, when the shocking truth dawned. We were ENJOYING it.

In fact, most New Zealanders have enjoyed an A and P Show at some time in their lives. It was a highlight of my childhood, though for a long time I was puzzled as to why Hay and Peas never seemed to have much to do with it.

The warmth and clamour, the vicarious thrills of the sideshows, the heady smells of candyfloss and cowdung and everywhere people spilling about in gay, gaudy profusion— well, it was Life.

It hasn't changed. It was all there at Helensville, offering us an orgy of nostalgia. People we didn't know actually spoke to us; the only disdainful expression I saw was on a horse which, crimped and preened for the occasion, refused to accept a common apple core. The only tension discernible flitted occasionally across the faces of small boys and girls parading their animals for the judges with intense care, or dancing Scottish reels as if devolution depended on it.

The comfortable amateurishness of an A and P Show is one of its most endearing qualities, yet there is no doubt that the skill which goes into preparing a bull for the ring, or an axe for the chop, or a jar of preserves for the produce shed, is something that we mere spectators can only surmise.

But it is nice to know that somewhere, in about a year's time some plump and rosy country wife will be contentendly pushing peaches into a jar ready for the show, while the rest of the world kills and plunders and devalues its currency.

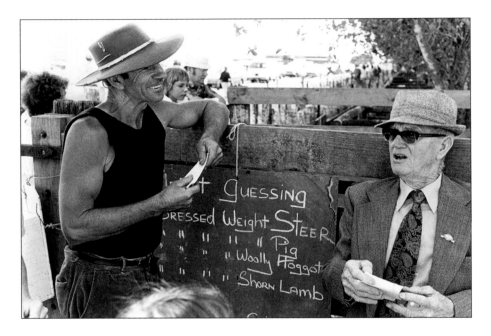

A Great Green Gusher

adrian blackburn

photographer:
bruce foster

22 september 1979

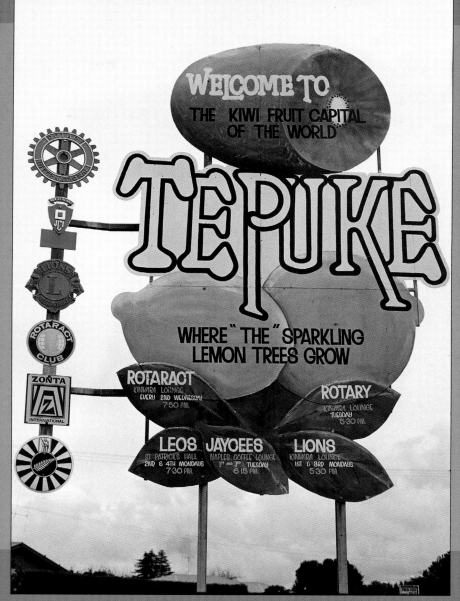

'Te Puke must be one of the richest little towns in the country because of what we've got around us.' Ian Johnson, garage proprietor and mayor of Te Puke.

'If anybody in Te Puke is not making money now they never will.' Peter Dixon, Te Puke home furnishing firm.

'I hope you're not going to write like they did in the *Star* about a year ago about how we're all millionaires down here. You'll be run out of town.' David Basham, editor of the *Te Puke Times*.

First, in the interests of balance—and of not being run out of the place—it's necessary to establish one thing about this pleasant central Bay of Plenty town: to say that you can't get a park there because every space is occupied by a 450SL Mercedes coupe would be a gross exaggeration.

But it *is* correct that commercial travellers, after weeks of depressed, declining country towns where even fusillades of shotgun blasts would threaten nothing more vital in the main street than War Memorial statuary, do complain when they reach Te Puke about having to park sometimes up to 50 yards from the shop they plan to honour.

That is really all they need complain of, for there is the smell of money here. Not that there's an obtrusive show of wealth. Jellicoe Street, Te Puke, broad as it may be, attractive as are the trees down its central strip, feels like a very normal town of 4000 souls going about their mutually advantageous business.

Absolutely normal, yes, until you suddenly realise that this confident, go-ahead place is strangely out of step with the rest of New Zealand.

The newly titivated, heavily stocked shops, the car yards whose stock can actually be seen week by week to change, the zzz-ing of skilsaws on framing timber in the new subdivisions above the business area, could all come straight from 1973.

Sales of kiwifruit will this year feed $20 million into Te Puke, a town of 4000 people, staff writer Adrian Blackburn reports on the berry boom and the fears of a bust.

Te Puke has escaped the recession.

The answer (again), lies in the soil, the deep, free-draining pumice soil in which the roots of *actinidia chinensis* rejoice, from which is drawn the nutriments for the miles of vines hemming in the borough, the kiwifruit placenta which this year will feed more than $20 million into the town.

The kiwifruit—Chinese gooseberry as he was—is a squat, ugly, little fellow with a brown fur coat who, if given a dollar or so in a German or Japanese greengrocers is ready, like Clark Kent, to strip dull outer cover to reveal the tangy green flesh of, yes, 'Superfruit'.

The overseas sales phenomenon of kiwifruit, pushed by clever promotion onto the tables of the very rich, has relied heavily on Te Puke.

Even two years ago Te Puke produced more than 75 per cent of world kiwifruit output and still justifies its claim to be the 'kiwifruit capital of the world'.

The harvest for the town has been rich. People have talked about the great green gusher. And it's no coincidence that in the glossy promotional photograph the little brown fellow is usually lit with a golden glow. There's no doubt that some individuals have made fortunes from the success of kiwifruit. And an established grower with a reasonable acreage can today make the sort of income many public companies would envy.

'Take the bloke who's selling 90,000 trays of kiwifruit this season,' said one Te Puke businessman. 'And there's a few of them around. At around $7 a tray that's more than $600,000 gross. Costs take about a third so he's left with something like $400,000 to play around with.'

Translate that income into value for the property which produced it and you can see why there are claims that Te Puke has 15 or more growers whose assets would exceed $1 million. If you reckon a top kiwifruit orchard in full production at about $50,000 an acre you can, in fact, see those claims as conservative.

In that light you might see the sale earlier this year by former rehab farmer Ashley Daley of Te Matai Road of 230 acres—160 acres planted in kiwifruit but not yet producing— for about $3.5 million as something of a bargain for the purchaser, Transport Nelson, the Newmans group.

More recently Pastoral Holdings paid $1.25 million for a Te Puke block of 31 acres.

Along with the companies have come city-based syndicates out to make a buck, or a million. Businessmen, doctors and accountants have got together to buy up dairy farms for planting, surveying them into notional subdivisions which they hope will become fact when the Tauranga County Council's new district scheme is released soon. Many individuals too have grabbed a few acres, frequently mortgaging themselves heavily.

Those seeing kiwifruit and Te Puke as synonymous have put spectacular pressure on land prices.

Take the experience of Bill Baldwin, a straightforward, hard-working ex-farmer who bought 16 acres of producing kiwifruit orchard up No 3 Road, heartland of the kiwifruit 'establishment', 13 years ago for £20,000.

Two years ago, seeking a few acres more, he was quoted $4000 an acre for bare unplanted land just east of the town— not top kiwifruit land. He decided to pay $5000 elsewhere, but today that $4000 land is now $10,000. And what would Baldwin get now for the 16-acre property which a buyer was ready to pay $500,000 for two years ago? Land agent Dick Gosling confirms that such a property would be worth about $1 million: 'Things have run away,' he says. 'There's a ton of demand and practically anything is counted as kiwifruit land.'

Even within the borough the owner of a few acres zoned residential has run kiwifruit T-bars through rather than subdivide.

Established growers reinvesting spare cash have helped push up prices. 'Some own up to five blocks now,' says Gosling.

Surprisingly few have really diversified, although some are into more conventional commercial investments and quite a number trying deer farming are buying up dairy farms a little way inland. The prime aim seems to be development, putting surplus dollars into projects which can later be sold for tax-free capital gain.

Major home improvements or big new homes have soaked up some money while the luxury yacht or launch, usually moored in Tauranga Harbour, seems to have taken precedence over luxury cars.

'We were a little disappointed things didn't take off sooner,' says Feo Stanton, whose Stanton Motors in Tauranga has agencies for some of the most exotic cars.

'But it does seem to have had an impact this year'— purchases this year have included Audis, Volvos, even a $74,500 Ferrari, the latter for Ashley Daley's son, and a number of Mercedes have been ordered.

Any Rolls? 'No,' says Campbell Fraser, Stanton sales manager. 'These Te Puke people are really very conservative. They would think a Rolls too ostentatious.'

There is some resentment among Te Puke retailers about money being spent 'out of the town'. Tauranga, 30 minutes' drive to the west, Auckland and Rotorua are the chief beneficiaries—although there are tales of matrons ringing each other to arrange a day's shopping spree in Sydney.

But one businessman is philosophical: 'There are only a few people, after all. The main thing is the spin-offs: the extra money wives earn working during the packing season or pruning.'

A typical family might earn an extra $1500 or so a year this way and sales of secondhand cars, home appliances and furnishings sparkle.

But the biggest business may be indirectly supplying growers, particularly during the capital intensive development stage. The only problem is to meet the demand.

Tauranga Timber Treatments, one of the bigger suppliers, has a 15- to 18-month delay on orders for tanalised pine posts to support vine frames.

'If we had 20,000 posts we'd sell them tomorrow,' the foreman says. Right. One big syndicate alone is said to need that number—at about $3.50 each. Posts have even been shipped from the South Island.

There's also a huge demand for six-metre poles to support artificial wind shelter fabric. About $1 million in orders are waiting.

There's a three-month wait for a builder. Nurseries providing shelter trees are expanding—one sold 50,000 trees to one syndicate—and naturally the big stock and station firms are reaping the dividends at every stage.

But there are some sour notes. 'Since they've had all this money some people I've known for many years have changed, and not for the better,' said a woman who has lived in the district since childhood. 'They're trying to out-do each other with what they get.'

Talking with townsfolk, there frequently appears a strong thread of resentment, of envy. Not many are as open-hearted as the accountant who said: 'It's hard work and most of these guys have grafted for a lot of years. Given the rewards are a bit awe-inspiring, but they've been prepared a long time ago to put their money where their mouth is. They've taken the risks.'

Newcomers may be taking even bigger risks. Some orchardists are ripping out mature citrus trees returning a good $3000 an acre per year, to plant the wonder fruit at a hoped-for return, some seven to ten years away, of $20,000 or more an acre. But others see warning signs.

Russell Baker, a third-generation Te Puke orchardist, is known as the local 'rebel' against the net of controls the Government threw over the industry when it established the Kiwifruit Marketing Licensing Authority in 1977. He decided two years ago not to extend his present 24 acres of kiwifruit.

He believes the 25 per cent export incentive—worth about $1 a tray to growers—has created an artificial return. (Naturally growers plan to fight the proposed 1983 removal of the incentive from Category A at present to only 2.8 per cent under Category G, known locally as trying to get their G into A.)

Baker believes that the best of the returns have been seen and that massive plantings both here and overseas will push the fruit from being an expensive delicacy into the volume fruit market, with a drop in real returns.

Baker is already diversifying into other subtropical crops.

A Tauranga accountant, a frequent adviser on kiwifruit investment, says: 'I'm very apprehensive about the whole

'Since they've had all this money some people I've known for many years have changed, and not for the better'

industry.' With people borrowing at high interest, the best part of 10 years' wait until full production, land prices three times as high as any other crop justifies and the likelihood of local labour shortages in the picking season forcing up wages, he is reluctant to encourage any but those well able to afford a shake-out.

'A lot of people are in it on a speculative basis to sell at a spectacular profit later. I question where the buyers will be for these properties at $500,000 and $1 million.'

Even the chairman of the Kiwifruit Marketing Licensing Authority, Roly Earp, himself a major grower, is adopting a lower-key approach than the industry has been used to in the past: 'Until now it has been very easy . . . Now we have to get out and market it. People coming into the industry have to be aware of this factor.'

Earlier this year it seems that even those blessed with the right to export the fruit—a tight little group of nine licence-holders—had to be awakened to this message.

At the start of the season, acting more like a cartel than competitors, they attempted to push on importers a price higher than the market was prepared to pay. Early sales were slow, the exporters backtracked, dropping their 'minimum export price' five per cent, and there is still a lot more kiwifruit unsold around the world than usual at this time of year.

Although this year's crop was a heavy one, much heavier crops will have to be disposed of in future as sales build up to the expected $186 million in 1990. This year's incident throws doubts on future marketing, but Earp is not prepared to concede that more exporters in the field might help.

'The present system with a limited number of exporters is working very successfully,' he says. New growers, crossing their fingers against a downturn in future returns, may soon be wondering whether he is right.

Established growers aren't worrying. 'The export price could drop by half and I'd still be doing well,' says one.

As for Te Puke, with new orchards starting earning every year, needing workers, needing services, it should remain sitting pretty, like its millionaires.

The Land at the End
of the Forecast

fiona kidman

31 july 1982

The Chatham Islands—no more than a name at the end of the weather forecast to most New Zealanders. Wellington writer Fiona Kidman spent a week in the Chathams earlier this year.

The land is strange and flat, the trees are bent towards the earth, the water is dark with swans. When Galway Kinnell wrote his line about a 'bitter beloved sea' he was not writing about the Chathams, but certainly he was writing about some place like it. It fits. The land and the sea around the islands are beloved by those who live here; to the stranger, it has that bitter desolate edge.

Like most people, I suppose, I have a desire to go to the ends of the earth. It seemed that if I were ever to begin, I should probably start at the end nearest to me, and for a long time the Chathams answered that need. 12 years ago I first spotted the famous Bristol Freighter service, Flight 131, loading to go to the Chathams. There were fishermen in thigh-boots, women laden with boxes of bread, pigs being loaded into the hold, and furniture and all manner of things which one takes for granted in daily life. In short, there was an air of departure for some remote and mysterious place.

I have had no reason to change my view over the years. It fascinates me still that only 700 people have their own weather forecast (usually, and often wrongly, for bad weather) broadcast several times a day, thereby regularly reminding the rest of New Zealand of their existence; yet few people have visited this part of the country.

And so, three hours and 770 kilometres out of Wellington, on the same Safe Air Bristol service (since replaced by Argosies), I see the islands for the first time. An outcrop of rock, a minute island, as flat, almost, as the sea itself, then Chatham Island, the larger of the two inhabited islands, stretching beneath us, so very much bigger than anticipated. It is difficult to tell where sea ends and land begins, and this is hardly surprising, for Chatham is virtually a ribbon of land surrounding the huge Te Whanga Lagoon. It has been described as being shaped rather like a Maori anchor stone, narrow in the waist and broad at either end. Pitt, the other occupied island, lies about 20 kilometres to the south-east and is small by comparison.

We are a strange mix on the bus which takes us into Waitangi. Some government servants, women with food supplies, a fisherman who has 'been to New Zealand' (I think I have come to visit a part of New Zealand but to the islanders New Zealand is New Zealand and they are from the Chathams—before many days have passed I too will talk of New Zealand, a place apart).

The air fills with cigarette smoke and the cut-down soft-drink cans nailed to the backs of the seats come into their own. Beside the road lie great white puddles of sand, gleaming in the darkish day, and although we can no longer see the sea, it is a reminder that it is just below the level of our vision, and that no part of the island is further than eight kilometres from the sea.

At the Hotel Chatham, I am installed in a pink and orange cell. The waves break almost beneath my window. There is a Gideon Bible and there is no key in the shining brass lock. I discover that it is rudeness on the islands even to consider that one might be necessary.

The hotel, centre of social life, is part of Waitangi, the biggest settlement, and the only one to have a general store. The prices are startling. Three kilos of sugar cost $3.80, 900 grams of cheese $4, a loaf of bread $1.40. There are some very dead cabbages selling for $1.30, and some lettuce-green bananas at $1.80 a kilo. To combat these prices, most islanders bring in six-monthly bulk supplies from wholesale distributors on the mainland.

Across the road from the store is the Post Office, and therein, the only facilities for obtaining money in the Chathams. There are no banks. There is a police station, though, and a courthouse, although Ian Robertson, who is policeman, probation officer, registrar, customs officer and scoutmaster all rolled into one, says it doesn't get much use. There's also the Chatham Islands County Council offices, the depot for Safe Air, a small museum, a hall where films are shown and dances sometimes held. Beyond the 'township' there are government settlements, where mostly MOW workers and radio operators live.

It is very quiet at the fish processing plant, the Chatham Island Packing Company, and beyond that again, the wharf. I have come in the off-season for crayfishing. Men are at work, though, on the annual servicing of their boats. But the quiet gets to you, and I am suddenly seized with panic. It is not unusual for new arrivals on the islands, but I am not to know that for the moment. Indeed, my fears are based on inescapable reality. No matter what happens to me here, barring severe accident or illness, in which case I would be taken out on a mercy flight, there is nothing I can do except stay here for the best part of a week. I am here, and I am alone, and for the moment I am frightened. More than anything, perhaps, I am frightened by the fact that, being a person who takes pride in her self-sufficiency, I am lonely.

At the hotel a bell is rung for dinner, restoring some sense of normality. Dinner is at six and that is that. Lunch is at 12.30 and breakfast at 7.30. If you miss, you've had it, and the nearest corner dairy is 800 kilometres away. They are implacable meal hours and while I am in the islands I become obsessive about my food, afraid that I will miss. Already I have a cache of oddly assorted food, purchased at considerable expense from the store, in my wardrobe—biscuits, tins of meat and bean salad.

Which is not to say that the Hotel Chatham sells you short on food. There is plenty of it, well-cooked, and bearing out the saying in the islands that 'when the tide's out, the table's set'. It is true, you need only walk to the edge of the sea, and the seafood is there for the taking.

If the hotel has any real problem, it is a frequent lack of alcohol. From time to time it is the archetypal pub with no beer, and when that happens the place rapidly runs dry of spirits as well, and there is even talk of strong men turning to Pimms. When things get too drastic between the six-weekly visits of the *Holmdale*, the ship that services the Chatham cargo route, the breweries charter a Bristol to relieve the drought with up to 225 dozen of beer—not a lot, when a good drinking man in the Chathams can sink a dozen in an hour. Or so they tell me.

I acquire a rental Land Rover, the only way to get around on the island. Nearly all vehicles apart from trucks are Land Rovers, although there are a few cars, rusting crates that the metalled roads have taken a heavy toll of. And there are abandoned cars by the dozen scattered across the landscape. When a car falls into too great a state of disrepair it seems that the easiest thing to do is just leave it where it is.

The plight of the young is one of the first things that strikes you here. There are virtually no teenagers on the Chathams, because nearly all adolescents go to the mainland for their secondary education. It is like a society with a gap in the middle of it.

On my first full day I talk to a class of Form II pupils at Te One School, as part of the Writers in Schools scheme. But I feel as if nothing really relates, that I am a curiosity from another planet. How big is a big building? What does a mountain look like? (The highest point on the Chathams is 273 metres.) What does an elevator actually feel like to ride on?

In return, I ask questions. Like, what are the best things about living in the Chathams?

Going hunting with my father. Eating wekas (it's legal here). And looking for shark teeth on Blind Jim.

Despite the disparity in our experiences, I make good friends there. When I walk along a beach a child will suddenly appear beside me and point out different varieties of dead eel strewn along the sand; birds are shown to me; introductions made to parents and grandparents. Some people who have lived on the mainland worry about their children being so friendly. They fear that when their children get there, they will be made vulnerable by their friendliness and openness.

Despite this, and despite the problems of intense homesickness, the majority of parents want their children to go to the mainland, to have a wider experience of life than the islands can offer. The departmental view, and one shared by MP Ann Hercus, whose Lyttelton constituency includes the islands, is that it would be impossible to equip and staff a school capable of providing the standard and curricular range of a mainland high school. A few pupils do stay and do high school work by correspondence but it is generally only moderately successful. Throughout the four schools on the two islands (with a combined roll of about 150 children) there are 13 doing correspondence now.

But so much is the lack of teenagers taken for granted that they are almost a nuisance when they come home for holidays. None of them know what to do with themselves any more and nobody really knows what to do with them.

The pupils at Te One, and apparently at the other three schools, boast a high rate of literacy. No television. But, say the teachers, you can notice a difference already in those with a video recorder at home.

The Chatham Islands are notable for a strong sense of community under quite exceptionally isolated conditions, but there are numerous subtle and not so subtle divisions. Nearly half of the 700 or so residents are government employees; the others are islanders, either by birth or permanent residence. There is nothing very subtle about that.

Government servants are seen as being the 'haves' and islanders as the 'have-nots'. Housing in the Chathams requires costly extras, such as power generators and septic tanks. Government employees are provided not only with free housing and furniture but all the amenities that islanders have to pay for.

On the other hand, government employees will tell you in unguarded moments that islanders are lazy, that they have the opportunity to be rich, and that they do not look after the things they do have.

Among the islanders themselves, there are the usual political divisions but also divisions caused purely by distance itself—children go away to high school and may never ultimately return—and between those who fish and those who farm. Against these, there are the bonds of generations of intermarriage. But even families have their differences.

Most islanders, as the result of intermarriage, are Maori or part-Maori, although one family, the Solomons, are the last known descendants of the Moriori, with distinctive features that set them apart from mainland Maoris. This is probably because Maori and European settlement took place within a relatively short space of time. By 1867 the whalers counted in their midst some 27 different races, including Germans, Spaniards, Portuguese, American Indians and Chinese. The assimilation of races was fast, and smooth skins and fine, often chiselled features are noticeable among the islanders.

They also have their own behaviour, and learning island etiquette is an essential requirement for getting to know people. Men, for instance, will always greet each other as 'bo' (or beau? Were there French sealers there too?), as in 'G'day bo, how you going bo?', but the women do not use it to each other.

The islanders are a curious blend, in their desire to catch up with the world on the one hand and to maintain their way of life on the other. The latter breeds an innate conservatism which sits uneasily alongside their claim to be predominantly Labour supporters. Indeed, the Prime Minister's visit last year is still talked about with something approaching reverence, though Ann Hercus says: 'Politics are different in the Chathams, because everyone who is a visitor, particularly an important one, is respected and welcomed. The islanders have no problem putting aside party affiliations.'

And the name of Norman Kirk is as alive as if he had been there yesterday. His huge signed photograph stares down at you with melancholy eyes at the entrance to the museum; he is, for the islanders, an irreplaceable memory.

But the other side still surfaces, and it is perhaps best illustrated by the reaction to the Springbok tour. Islanders are rugby-crazy, and the tour appears to have had no opponents at all, with the exception of the resident Roman Catholic priest. He went over to Pitt and preached a sermon condemning the tour. On the Saturday afternoon a group were sitting in a corrugated tin shed listening to one of the tests. Father Frank picked up a stick and started rattling it against the corrugations to drown out the commentary. He was driven off when shots were fired.

Some say now that it was all a bit of a joke, others that it was why he was replaced, while back in the hotel some of the visitors say over dinner that they think it is the bravest story to come out of the tour.

But they do not say it in the bar. And for now, it is Saturday night in the Hotel Chatham, and the birthday of Ursula Crack, who runs the hotel with her husband George. The house guests carry the party on into the small hours.

In my narrow room, when it has ended, I lie and listen to the sea. Through the paper-thin walls the man from the Education Department snores gently to my left, while on my right a P&T lad calls out in his sleep. Chathams time is three-quarters of an hour ahead of the mainland, and this is the first place in the world where the day begins. I decide to stay awake and be the first person in the world, for this day at least, to watch the day break.

David Holmes is one of the older and most respected residents. He has spent the last five to 10 years recording different facets of the Chathams in clear concise prose. He has seen two of the three tidal waves which have swept the islands within living memory, seen people come and go. He and his wife live in a rambling kauri house, built exactly a century ago by a Captain Hood, as a homestead and shop in one. It is a Chatham landmark and for the centenary party anyone who wants to will be able to come and see it.

Holmes spent 50 years on the county council, 14 of them as chairman. He and Fred Lanauze, who followed him as chairman for a six-year term, dwell on the problems faced by farmers in the islands.

Land ownership problems and the absence of a rating system have contributed largely, they say, to a lack of interest

I decide to stay awake and be the first person in the world, for this day at least, to watch the day break.

in the development of farmland. The confused state of original Maori land ownership made it virtually impossible to collect what was owing, so a county levy on all goods imported into and exported from the islands was introduced in 1936, and it was only last year that land rating began. The cost of the levies to the farmers has, in itself, been a deterrent (for instance, if you include the price of handling across the wharf, plus transport costs, it takes $130 simply to get a bale of wool to the mainland). Despite this, there was a postwar farming boom, and the high prices of wool in the early 50s encouraged the development of farming. But much of what had been achieved was lost when the cray boom began.

There is also the problem of water retention and storage, for despite the Chathams' miserable weather forecasts, they have an average rainfall of only 890 mm. And thanks to indiscriminate burning-off, particularly of the land known as the 'clears', and the introduction of pigs, Chatham Island at least (Pitt has not been so badly affected) has lost all its natural vegetation. Even the Chatham Island lily which once covered the islands is now a rarity. There is fern, mile after mile of it, and to re-grass and fertilise properly is an undertaking of such expense that it is difficult to see how high production can be achieved without enormous government subsidies.

But the Romney sheep on the islands are a particularly good strain, and in some demand for breeding on the mainland. There is a meatworks on the road to Owenga. 'It's the salvation of the people here,' says David Holmes, 'if they could only see it.'

Fred Lanauze thinks that perhaps too many of the islands' affairs are governed by the mainland. 'They tell us how to do things,' he says, 'but they don't even bother to come here. I don't think they always understand the issues involved. I'm not saying the Government isn't spending money here, but I don't know whether it's the right way. You know, schemes are introduced to help farmers, but by the time we get to hear of it, the scheme's finished six months before. You ask what assistance you can get, but by the time your application gets processed it's too late. I reckon we're about 80 or 90 years behind the mainland here.'

Nothing symbolises the frustrations of the relationship with the mainland more than the vexed matter of the air service.

When the airstrip was begun it was designed for Fokker Friendships. It is not long enough for a fully laden Argosy, but that is the plane that has taken over from the old Bristol Freighters, and the Argosy itself is now obsolete. Indeed, it is said that there are now only nine operational Argosies left in the world. In addition to its excessive weight, it has had to be re-designed with a special internal capsule to carry passengers; at present it is operating only weekly, rather than twice-weekly, out of Christchurch; there has been no Wellington service for the past few months, though it is due to resume next month; and of course fares have gone up—from $356 to $400 for a return flight from Christchurch now. The Chathams, desperate for a more up-to-date air service, are apparently having an antique one foisted on them after the building of the modern airport which they turned out so enthusiastically to see opened by the Prime Minister only last year.

The same problem of isolation drives would-be home-owners to near desperation. The cost of everything is so high, because of transport costs, that a house which might cost $30,000 on the mainland, a modest dwelling by today's standards, will cost $70,000 in the Chathams. Loans and basic materials are extremely difficult to obtain.

Kaingaroa village, for instance, looks like a wild west shanty town, some 30 or 40 houses built cheek by jowl. At the end of the road, they run out into little more than structures of the packing-case variety. The conditions have to some extent been brought about because the people have not been able to obtain titles to the land, so there is no point in their erecting houses of any value. It is not uncommon here for one person to own a house and another to own the land it is built on, but the social consequences of the problem are particularly severe at Kaingaroa.

Rob Leathley, who runs the fish processing plant at Kaingaroa, is the third manager in as many seasons, and he and the people who work for him do not appear to be entirely in sympathy with each other. He seems uneasy and dispirited. 'The place went back when all the footballers died,' he says. 'It just never recovered.'

The extraordinary story of the lost football team is that, in 1936, 13 young men set out by boat for Waitangi for a game of football, two of the team electing to ride overland. The boat was never seen or heard of again.

Yet such is the obsession with football on the two islands that a boat will still set out to Pitt in a two-metre swell if numbers are needed to make up a team. If there is an appreciation of danger, it is not dwelt upon too deeply. One will survive, or not.

For all the squalor of much of the village, I am invited into an immaculate house for afternoon tea, one of the few solid dwellings, and we sip from fine china and admire the largest collection of Howard Morrison records I have ever seen.

We return via Blind Jim again, and this time Ursula Crack and I stop to hunt for the famous fossilised shark teeth in Te Whanga Lagoon. They were laid down under the sea in the Eocene period, and now, as the limestone is eroded, the teeth are washed up by the waves, ranging in colour from black to pale blue. We find a particularly good blue.

The true feeling of timelessness which I had been told to expect on the islands has not really overtaken me until now. It is not just the age of these remains, which we are picking up in small handfuls, but the place itself. Ursula moves away from me and suddenly I am alone, but not lonely, on the Chathams, with water and a darkening sky, knee-deep in the ancient lagoon. It does not seem particularly important whether the Bristol comes to collect me or not the following day. It doesn't seem to matter whether I go home or not.

But the plane does come and I join the diverse assortment of people straggling onto the plane—the man from the department; a shepherd leaving the islands, complete with saddle, cowboy hat and five dogs; a couple who packed at half an hour's notice to be with a dying relative, afraid of missing the last plane out for a week; fishermen going on holiday during the off-season.

One of the crew hands out the morning newspaper from Christchurch. A newspaper. For a moment I am excited, then I put it down. Tonight there will be another newspaper waiting at home, the 6.30 news on television, I'll wake up to *Morning Report*; all the news the mind can assimilate, and more.

For now, I have a handful of shark teeth 55 million years old in my jeans pocket, a carton of frozen paua left at the depot as a parting present from a local, and a few seconds left to look at those islands, set in their 'bitter, beloved sea'.

City with a Heart
(but no centre)

tony reid
photographer: bruce connew
16 october 1982

The unusual statistics could attract tourists. This is New Zealand's fastest-growing city and, by now, probably the largest. It is claimed that only Los Angeles covers a bigger area. There is also a growing conviction that the city's future might be the measure of our ability to order, stabilise and civilise sudden population growths.

Yet Manukau remains an 'invisible' city. As you travel southwards through New Zealand fewer and fewer people know about the place. Many have never heard of it. And, if you ask the South Auckland locals where they live, the reply will probably be 'Auckland' or the name of their suburb. Not Manukau.

The tourists don't come. How could they enjoy a city that doesn't really seem like a city at all? There is no built-up area containing high buildings lining busy, downtown streets. Plenty of urban problems but very little of the facilities or central city sophistication.

The tourist would drive through mile after mile of slightly depressed, depressing suburbs. Lines of little boxes on a seemingly endless plain. The outsider feels he is always on the verge of arriving at a focus, some central point that might define the city's flavour. The expectation is not fulfilled.

True, Manukau does have a commercial heart. Appropriately it is next to the southern motorway that traverses this region and magnetises the ribbons of suburbs accompanying its progress. You are unlikely to find downtown without a car and local knowledge. The commercial centre is, of course, as unusual as the other unusual aspects of Manukau—a great slab of shops and offices slapped down in the middle of green countryside.

Acres of carpark, no conventional streets and, near the country's most architecturally futuristic local body building, a giant, covered, air-conditioned shopping 'city'. Your eye travels across country grassland to this huge symbolic cash register sitting smugly within it.

Stand in the centre of this shopping complex and shops form very distant horizons at each end. It is only five years old and city manager Ron Wood still laughs at the reaction of his mates during the planning stages. The wags gave Ron a hard time. 'See you downtown,' they would chortle. 'Meet you at the corner of Main Street.' Everyone knew you would be standing next to a milking shed in farmland.

Wood, a sensible, unflappable man didn't mind the gibes. His council bought the land for $1000 an acre and it is now worth about $150,000 an acre. He allows a quiet smile of triumph.

Indeed, the Manukau City Council has always needed big ideas and the nerve to take big risks.

It was formed as the administrative expression of a need to manage Auckland's suburban sprawl towards the Bombay Hills. The 550 sq km of suburbs and flat countryside extends from Otahuhu to Papakura and from Mangere to Orere on the Firth of Thames.

In the decade from 1966 the population increase was equivalent to the size of Tauranga. Only five years ago Manukau issued a million dollars worth of building permits a week and catered for 25 new residents a day.

In those early days the council struggled to cope with this astonishing growth. Group developers created production line new towns; there were pressures to turn the local authority into a super real estate agency presiding over enormous housing markets.

The people who migrated into these outer, outer suburbs of Auckland? Executives not quite ready for Remuera inhabited such *nouveau riche* enclaves as Pakuranga and Bucklands Beach. Millions of dollars poured into suburbs geared to the god of ostentation; these new, huge homes seemed desperately eager to proclaim their expense.

The country's most architecturally futuristic local body building.

Mock Tudor, Mock Spanish, American colonial, ranchstyle, split level—cost often seemed the only common factor in an extraordinary mixture of architectural styles. These days the wealth is even more droolingly displayed and makes North Shore spa pool territory look slightly tatty. At Half Moon Bay, for instance, one of the southern hemisphere's finest marinas caters for an estimated $30 million of boats.

But, away from such areas of Manukau's coast, life has never been glamorous. During the great population influx an archetypal new resident was poorly educated, coloured, hard-up and young. He had been dispossessed by changing social and employment patterns. Rural Maoris coming to the big smoke, Pacific Islanders seeking a thicker paypacket, people squeezed out of such inner city areas as Ponsonby—these are the citizens who arrived before many community facilities to make life bearable in the South Auckland urban sticks.

Otara, Block One. Ron Wood looks weary at the memory.

During the early 1970s Otara epitomised Manukau's problems and became the country's most infamous suburb. Violence, vandalism, delinquency, poverty, alcoholism, family misery, no suburban spirit—the list of community charges seemed endless.

'But we were learning together,' says Wood. 'Everyone, including the council, was working flat out to solve problems. Heads down and tails up.'

The council struggled to cope and so did the residents. The latter learned that self help was imperative —those in suburbs that had the least must now learn to do the most for themselves.

They organised, demanded and found their council eager to listen. Manukau evolved 'shared responsibility schemes'. The locals organised ideas, enthusiasm and one quarter of the money for urgently needed amenities. The Manukau City Council provided a further quarter and lent the financial balance without interest over 15 years.

Now Manukau is no longer considered a plethora of Auckland dormitory suburbs. Indeed, it is rapidly becoming the region's most important, self-contained industrial area. Population growth is slowing. And there has been a big investment in special community assistance—the council, for instance, currently supports 83 projects offered by the Labour Department.

'But nothing really changes,' reflects Wood calmly. 'You name it and we've got it. Always did. Racially, socially . . .

'Look, there are more Polynesians in Manukau than in Rotorua. And there's far, far more problems. Beating them? You're crazy if you think you can beat a problem. Out here it just turns into another problem.'

A visit to Otara in 1982 confirms this judgement. It is now a suburb comparatively rich in community amenities and many are the result of residents' own initiative.

But the social problems remain in more diluted form and rising unemployment (a second generation of jobless is not uncommon) deepens difficulties. Some European social workers talk of adolescents who are almost illiterate, have never worked and have no desire to work; some European teachers talk of Maori primary school students who have a pathetically limited vocabulary in either language.

Yet there is real local pride among some of the teenagers. They wouldn't live anywhere else but Otara. The kids are direct, tough, street-wise and articulate—extremely resourceful and supportive of one another. They have discarded many of the cultural values that sustain their parents and, in a striking number of cases, they have also turned away from the traditional Otara affection for the East Tamaki Tavern.

A recent Education Department report on Otara states: 'A third culture is emerging, of children who are neither

Yet there is real local pride among some of the teenagers. They wouldn't live anywhere else but Otara.

Pacific Islanders, nor rural Maoris, but not New Zealanders as the term is generally understood.'

Manukau City's 'urban tribalism' exists against a background of growing contrasts between white and coloured, rich and poor. Predominantly European suburbs have promoted the idea of a breakaway eastern city; European people living in Mangere and Otara 'bus' their children out to Otahuhu College; many people of similar outlook are moving out of Otara and there are sighs of relief on both sides.

Although one Manukau councillor has called this trend 'apartheid by natural selection' Wood isn't deeply distressed. 'At one stage "pepperpotting" was all the rage; to mix people of different racial and economic backgrounds in the same street. We didn't try the impossible and legislate for that sort of thing.

'It's no good telling people where to live. Instead, we try to get alongside all sorts of groups, listen and be guided by their varying aspirations. The worst thing is to impose patterns—to rely on bylaws and regulations.

'It's so easy for local bodies to go that way. But much more sensible to listen to what people are saying and help them get what they want.

'That's what we are doing out here. Everyone is different. Everyone wants to live in different ways. They will, anyway.'

Coromandel:
The Peninsula War

bruce gooding
photographer: bruce connew
4 December 1982

Kuaotunu, circa 1896, was one of those booming, bustling, gold-rush locales that legends are made of. Four pubs, as many boarding-houses, makeshift dwellings galore, up to a thousand residents at its peak. Stamper batteries were working at least 10 different claims in this Coromandel coastal area as opportunists chased after that elusive treasure, gold.

Visit Kuaotunu these days and that seems but a faded memory. There's little more than a store, a garage, a petrol pump, a hall, a scattering of country houses, a line of seaside baches.

But this could all change. If Goldmines of New Zealand Ltd gets its way, it will be all go for Kuaotunu once again. The company, an offshoot of the South Africa-based multinational Anglo-American, wants to mine the gold left untouched by last century's pick-and-shovel brigade. Goldmines has identified a gold-bearing ore resource of at least 20 million tonnes in seven different areas on the Kuaotunu Peninsula, half-an-hour's drive north of Whitianga. The company is seeking prospecting rights over 2900 hectares of country stretching inland from the famed Blackjack road on the coast and including the scenic reserve immediately inland.

At three grams of gold to the tonne—said by the company to be the minimum yield needed for mining to be economic— the resource is worth, at the gold price current at time of writing, a think-big style $1200 million. But although Goldmines of NZ—and Anglo-American—would love to tap this wealth, their efforts are being frustrated by a well-organised legal campaign mounted by environmental groups and supported by Kuaotunu residents who are almost unanimously opposed to the scale of mining needed to economically extract the widely dispersed resource. Earlier this year at a public meeting, local residents voted 74 to 2 against Goldmines' proposals. Many local people are helping to

A multinational company wants to mine the gold left over from last century; the anti-mining lobby is determined to stop them. Staff writer Bruce Gooding reports that the two factions are shaping up for a long battle.

raise money so the Environmental Defence Society (EDS) can continue its long-running battle against mining companies like Goldmines of NZ.

Goldmines of New Zealand is a Nelson-registered company in which Australian Anglo-American now has 95 per cent interest, the balance being held by a subsidiary of Brierley Investments. Another New Zealand company, Cue Energy Resources NL, funds 20 per cent of Goldmines' exploration budget. Australian Anglo-American is in turn owned by three giant South African corporations, one of which is Anglo-American of South Africa (Harry Oppenheimer's group of South African companies, which includes Anglo-American and de Beers, has assets of $20,000 million. For comparison, Fletcher Challenge's reserves total $613 million.)

For three years, the EDS has been fighting Goldmines on legal grounds in a bid to stop the company winning prospecting licences over Kuaotunu land it has already explored. The latest round in the saga took place before Judge Patterson in the Thames District Court where objections to the granting of three prospecting licences to the company were heard. Judge Patterson is expected to present his report on the matter to the Minister of Energy, Mr Birch, who has the final say as to whether the prospecting rights should be granted. Environmentalists are saying that the judge's—and the minister's—decision is critical because in this instance the original Mining Act, and not the amended version, applies. This means that if Goldmines is given a prospecting licence, they can automatically gain a mining licence.

The anti-mining lobby has attacked Goldmines' proposals—in court and elsewhere—on a number of fronts. Large-scale mining, say the opponents, would do irreversible damage to the area's exceptional scenic character while the threat of pollution from tailings dumps would jeopardise the good name of the export-oriented coastal fishery in the area. The mere existence of a mine without any pollution would, says the EDS, be a bad enough deterrent to overseas buyers of the fish and scallops. But an actual poisoning instance, the chance of which the anti-faction says Goldmines can't rule out entirely, could ruin a $10 million export industry overnight.

A further plank to the anti-mining case—and one not pursued during the hearings—is the claim by Peninsula Watchdog spokespeople and others that it has not been proven that mining will benefit the country economically, given the multinational background of Goldmines NZ Ltd.

In framing its environmental case against Goldmines in the latest hearings, EDS drew heavily on a report prepared by Goldmines' own geologists for Anglo-American following the company's exploration of the area. The company was forced to produce this report after the EDS filed a writ of discovery in November last year. The report confirmed that a large-scale operation, whether open-cast or block-caving, would be needed to render the project economic.

EDS called 11 witnesses to give evidence on the environmental impact of large-scale mining. These included admissions from the Commission for the Environment, the Thames-Coromandel District Council—which had called for a moratorium on the issuing of licences until a planning study had been carried out—and the Hauraki Regional Water Board. Goldmines called two witnesses of its own, including a company geologist, but presented no evidence disputing the EDS witnesses' contentions.

Goldmines director John Lawrey vigorously discounts the value of the opposing witnesses' submissions. Lawrey writes off, for example, evidence relating to the effect of mining on the fishery as 'conjecture unrelated to fact'. Representatives of both the Fishing Industries Board and local fishermen supported the EDS's contention that fish and scallop exports could be disadvantaged by the existence alone of mining in the area. Any additional input of mercury would raise the mercury-level on the fishery above World Health Organisation standards, the court was told.

Lawrey says people forget that the best brains in the world would be designing the tailings dams. 'Anglo-American would just have to make sure there would be no pollution to keep its good reputation,' he says. He claims there's no shred of evidence that mining has affected fish life, 'and it's very unlikely that it would ever do so.'

Anti-mining lobbyist Mike Donoghue, a marine scientist and fisherman, seizes on this last point.

'The fact that pollution may be "very unlikely" doesn't

support the company's case at all. It would only need one spillage and exports from the whole Coromandel fishery could be finished.' Donoghue and EDS executive officer Gary Taylor both say the mining company's assurances here shouldn't be accepted at face value.

'We just can't believe they'll do the job properly,' says Taylor. 'And even if they think they're doing the right thing with the tailings, they can't guarantee that there won't be a spillage. Could any dam be guaranteed to cope with a 10-day Coromandel rain?'

Lawrey is as dismissive of other EDS evidence relating to the sensitive, unstable nature of the land at Kuaotunu.

'We have the resources to plan this thing properly to meet all environmental objections.'

He claims it would be in the interests of the environment movement if the oppposition was dropped and Anglo-American allowed in. 'If we are forced to abandon our plans, it's highly likely that the mining option will be taken up by a smaller company without the same ability to do a good job environmentally.'

The EDS also called evidence relating to the planning implications of giving Goldmines the green light. Taylor: 'We considered the government was engaging in ad hoc decision making without giving regard to the cumulative effects of granting these privileges. The Commission for the Environment questioned the wisdom of proceeding with a massive industrial complex in a rural recreational area. The Thames-Coromandel District Council repeated its call for a moratorium (Mr Birch told the council later by letter there was no provision in the Mining Act for a moratorium). The Hauraki Regional Water Board added its weight to the council's call for a full study.

Mr Lawrey says the company cannot say what their mine

'. . . they can't guarantee that there won't be a spillage. Could any dam be guaranteed to cope with a 10-day Coromandel rain?'

or mines would look like until prospecting reveals the true resource. 'But if Anglo is involved, it will be a sizeable one.' He concedes that he did say once that 2000 people would be employed at the mine and 'downstream' of it 'but it was a mistake to say this'. Again, he can't be precise on this at this stage. Asked whether he thinks the country will benefit economically from such a mine in view of Goldmines' 95 per cent South African backing, Lawrey says he can 'only generalise' on a mine's economic worth at this stage. He points to the 'horrifying general economic scenario that is developing here', and says 'here is a great chance to diversify into something productive'.

What's to stop 95 per cent of the proceeds leaving the country? That's ludicrous, he says. All countries, says Lawrey, have to tell the Overseas Investment Commission that if required they will put a 50 per cent New Zealand content into any situation. 'I'm almost certain a mine will be on this basis.' He accepts, though, that there is no specific 50 per cent requirement now.

He admits the tax basis for mining companies is better than that for a normal industrial operation. 'But this is because the risks are so horrendous.'

'Everyone knows the government will get their slice out of it. Any time you earn a dollar in this country, a lot flows to the government.'

The fact that the world depression is continuing, says

Black rocks concealing gold? Kuaotunu Beach's pristine foreshore is threatened by the prospect of large-scale gold mining.

Lawrey, is an added reason for the government to quickly sanction mining. Mining could help New Zealand 'ride out the depression' since it is historically proven that the price of gold holds well in hard times.

Despite his lack of hard economic evidence, Lawrey claims the mining would be in the best interests of New Zealanders generally. 'It's arrogant for the small number of objectors to put their interests first.' Doesn't he accept that the opposition to Goldmines' application in and around Kuaotunu is far more widespread than merely a small fringe? Yes, he concedes, but doesn't it come down to the best interests of the country as a whole? 'I really do question the political motives of the organised opposition.'

'We're not anti-development per se, if that's what he's getting at,' replies Mark Tugendhaft, Peninsula Watchdog spokesman, when told of Lawrey's latter remark. 'We'd simply prefer some development that is compatible with the area—like tourism or horticulture. Heavy industry is not on because its pollution—or its threat of possible pollution—will affect these other developments.'

Tugendhaft says the scale of operations mentioned to date—20 million tonnes—would be a minimum only. 'Would they stop at that if they found a lot more? Of course they wouldn't.' Tugendhaft thinks the government should foster New Zealand's strengths by manufacturing products from resources that can be compatibly exploited. This would enable the country to compete abroad.

'And it would be thinking big. Thinking small is handing over to the multinationals.

'There's enough evidence from overseas to show that the multinationals will use us mercilessly to their own ends. If we allow them in to mine for gold, we'll be allowing in the worst of the industrial world—the users of the most capital and the providers of the least numbers of jobs. Why is the government so totally negative about New Zealand potential to organise her own development?'

Tugendhaft and Taylor bemoan the fact that mineral development seems to be proceeding on an ad hoc basis.

'Why wasn't mining on the think-big project list?' says Tugendhaft.

The result is that each area faced with mining has to defend itself also on an ad hoc basis.

'There is no body creating a policy of wisest use of resources.' At the same time, he alleges, the Mines Division and the mining industry are all pushing to facilitate mining. The expense is falling on people—like those in Kuaotunu—because no organisation has the power to counter the push of the government.

How do Lawrey and Goldmines feel about their chances of proceeding at Kuaotunu? Lawrey replies that if this 'horrendous' series of court hearings goes on and on, Anglo-American could lose enthusiasm.

'But environmentalists would be the losers if a smaller company got in there instead.' Goldmines had already spent up to $300,000 in the area.

And do Taylor and the EDS feel pessimistic? 'No, for the first time I really think we're going to stop them,' he says.

'We're confident despite the fact that the amended Mining Act does not apply and the minister can still do what he likes on getting the judge's report.

'But even if we lose out at this stage, we have a number of legal options left.'

Taylor hotly denies that EDS is simply stalling. 'This would be quite improper and would place us in severe jeopardy. If you don't have bona fide reasons for litigating, you

Why is the government so totally negative about New Zealand potential to organise her own development?

can have an award of costs against you that can throw you out of existence.'

Taylor says EDS hopes through the legal process to get some recognition of the logic of its argument.

'We think our case is irrefutable.

'The issue raises the very important question of whether a community in New Zealand can have some direction over what happens in its district, a community in this case that is virtually at one in terms of its attitude.

'It's just desperate tactics to say we're just a handful of stirrers standing in front of necessary development.'

Deep and Singing Silences

From silent land to silent space, with the Mackenzie dogs between.

geoff chapple
photographer: geoff chapple
20 october 1984

The Maniototo—the plain of blood. We were 70 kilometres in from the coast, in country where you expect nothing but the roll of Central Otago's hills, and we came down on the Maniototo stunned by the extent of the flat-land.

Its history is this. The plain was named for an old Maori battle. It was opened to European run-holders in the 1850s, a vast plain of ample ground-cover, streams, swamps and fog. The runs were overgrazed, and, to procure green-shoot feed, overburned. Scab-weed took hold, wind erosion, rabbits. The plain became desolate.

Elevated above it to the south is the Styx Valley, a tussocky flat dotted with grotesque rock formations, but also a natural platform where the waters of the Taieri River might be dammed and piped to the plain below. Yet the Maniototo's whole history seems like a revenge for the original disturbance, and the irrigation scheme of the 1980s was no exception, triggering a political storm with its cost over-runs.

It was evening. The cloud ceiling was low and seemingly as dense and level as the plain itself. Pyres from the spring burn-off and creeping edges of fire in the fields sent up screens and pillars of smoke which joined earth to sky. We stopped, and on the instant were transfixed by a dark magic. Partly it was the dissolution of the light, partly the mountains and rock-encrusted ranges which enclose the plain on every side and give to it a quality of brooding introspection. Partly it was the lowering cloud, but it was also a sense of withdrawal.

For the fires burned alone. Neither there nor amidst the tree-belts which mark the Maniototo homesteads was there a sign of life. We saw no one, felt only a single pulse of the inland plain, compounded on the laws of fire and smoke and compression and absence. Laws which seemed in that moment less than benign. For an instant we quivered in the jaws of it, then scudded on to the safety of Ranfurly's lights 10 kilometres distant.

Perhaps we were mistaken. Morning gave us Ranfurly, a town of single-storey buildings laid out at the plain's centre, flat as a flag, intersected by wide streets the farmers drive into—and out of—at speed. We drove south and stopped to watch shearing at the Stonehenge station. Beads of sweat dripped from the brow of shearers and wool peeled off the merinos in a white carpet. From the sheep dripped beads of blood.

South until we climbed to the Styx Valley. Here the road makes a terminal circuit around a small swampy plain where 10 households, five either side of the Upper Taieri River, stare at each other's chimney-smoke.

The map shows one road going on from there. A dotted line warns that it's unmetalled, winding up and over the Rock and Pillar Range and on across the Lammermoors, some of the most inhospitable highlands in the south. This is the old Dunstan Road, originally a gold trail on which the 19th-century miners 'rushed' between the strikes of the Maniototo and the Clutha Valley. The most direct route, but shelterless and subject to storm—the most dangerous. Some of the miners died on these highlands.

You had to be motivated: gold, or this set of wavy lines on the map, with tufts. This intriguing label: *The Great Moss Swamp*. The Dunstan Road goes up the Rock and Pillar Range and across the Lammermoors—right past it.

One thousand metres up, and climbing. The bonnet was pointed at blue sky. Cobb and Co—the real one—once used this road, and anything Cobb horses could pull, a Bedford 214 could pull better.

A snow-bank lay half across the road. The spring melt was on, and it leaked a sheen of water across the clay. *Gee-up!* Our back wheels skidded, and we had a moment of wishing they were big and spoked—something you could put your shoulders to. We came on for another try, and stood churning in one spot. Farewell Great Moss Swamp, unless—a quick check on the map showed the swamp maybe 12 kilometres in from there—you walked it.

Blue sky and silence. The hills were like dunes except for the bolt of rock which stuck up through every smooth summit. The Rock and Pillar Range. Its straight-grained schist has a propensity to break in angles across the grain—to break in the angle of a hood or cowl.

One hour in: blue sky and a silent watcher on every hill. From the rock promontories, the impression of hooded surveillance was distinct.

Two hours in: the glint of a high-altitude jet needle and its thin trail. On the ground, this discarded Speights beer-can. I'd begun to seize anything man-made, even litter, with inordinate affection. Even to seek out human evidence. High on a rock prominence, a large bottle. I detoured up steep tussock to investigate, and the bottle waited motionless before sprouting wings and gliding away. Hawk!

And no sign of the Great Moss Swamp. Just pure sky, pure silence, and in every gully, the snow, pure white. I was feeling

Every new experience reels a new emotion to the surface. I wanted that — a great soggy green emotion, hectares in extent.

fine—no I wasn't. A pigeon-hole of the mind disgorged this fact: the last and most dangerous phase of exposure is signalled by the victim who pushes any rescuer away. *No! I'm fine, fine.* Sailing at last out beyond human boundaries . . . I had a moment's insight into the minds of the miners who sat and died in the region. Gold. The singing silence. The cold. I had the feeling starlight in a place like this would be dreadful—wonderful. More to the point, cloud was starting to roll across the Lammermoors ahead, and I had no confidence in my ability to judge the weather.

But the swamp. Every new experience reels a new emotion to the surface. I wanted that—a great soggy green emotion, hectares in extent.

Another half-hour, and I got the emotion. Sheer disappointment. Maybe it was the wrong time of year, but the swamp looked like an ordinary blue lake. I checked it closer in, then turned and followed my footprints all the way back along the Dunstan Road.

We came out of the Maniototo through Danseys Pass. The signs say LIGHT TRAFFIC ONLY. NO CARAVANS. WINDING ROAD. But if you want to avoid the main highways in the south, you come to ignore signs like that. The sheep trucks go over the pass because it's the short route between the Maniototo and the Waitaki Valley, and so did we, choosing night for the advance warning of headlights coming the other way. Leaning rock-faces on one side, and on the other a margin of tussock, brightly defined against the blackness which falls away below; but we went through without difficulty.

In the morning we followed Highway 83 up past the big hydro stations of the Waitaki Valley. Waitaki itself, Aviemore, Benmore—all with their artificial lakes coloured swimming-pool aquamarine, and with willows breaking into green leaf at their shores. The colours stood in startling contrast to the barren mountains which surround the lakes.

At Omarama we turned right onto Highway 8, headed through to South Canterbury and the Mackenzie Country. The Mackenzie story is well-known: he was a Gaelic-speaking shepherd apprehended while driving 1000 stolen sheep into the little-known interior, 1855. But the legend is secured as much by the shepherd's dog, Friday.

Friday was said to have had her tongue slit to stop her barking, to have the ability to receive orders and to carry them out hours later when her master was safely distant. After Mackenzie's jailing, there are tales she was hanged or shot as a witch.

False stories perhaps, but the pain of separation— Mackenzie in jail, his dog outside it—was true at least. And true or false, dog legends are part of the Mackenzie Country. There was Friday, and there were also the borderers' dogs which worked weeks without human company, patrolling the boundaries of fenceless runs against straying sheep, the dog that killed wekas and brought them miles to its incapacitated master . . . the list is long.

We drove down a straight highway for an hour, and into Twizel. By the time we drove out, I had added the dogs of Twizel to the Mackenzie Country dog legend.

For we got lost in Twizel trying to find the shopping centre. The claim would probably sound absurd to the 5000 Twizel residents, but we got lost and were harried by small dogs. Twizel is like a big flat suburb and at some time a fashion for lap dogs must have swept it. We blundered through it, out of scale amidst unitary rows of 10-perch sections, fibrolite-sheet houses, and into streets which turned into cul-de-sacs too small for our turning circle. The dogs sensed it. Every second section seemed to launch a wheel-biting terrier,

a pomeranian, a pekinese . . . we came out gunning the motor, not caring finally if we squashed them flat as wafers, but the dogs of Twizel are also quick.

We spent the night at a nearby motor-camp. In the morning, a retired man emerged from his caravan across the way and lobbed a ball 20 metres across the turf. A Sydney silkie watched the man with static curiosity, while a second dog, a pomeranian, ambled about aimlessly. The man went and retrieved the ball, threw it again: same sequence.

I went across. The performance of the Sydney silkie, Flash, I was assured, was disturbed by the presence of the camp dog, Fluffie. Were it not for Fluffie, Flash was a gun at ball retrievals.

Bevan Mears is a permanent resident at the camp. He'd been a jockey, a good one, he told me, not great, but good, with wins in the Grand National and other major races to his credit. More recently he'd worked on the Upper Waitaki construction. Then he'd retired and gone down to Christchurch, but he lasted there only a month. He was a backblocks' person. The Mackenzie Country, the caravan with its TV aerial, and Flash.

'He's put a few grey hairs on my head, this one, eh,' said Bevan Mears, pointing unselectively to a headful. 'They told me when I bought him they were wanderers. He'll go for miles—right up to the tip between here and Twizel. I don't know what he goes up there for, but I go after him. Now imagine looking for a dog like that in tussock country.'

It was true—a fair description of Flash to call him an animated tussock.

'It worries me, eh. People tell me he's quick, but the cars come along these roads at speeds you wouldn't believe and there's plenty of quick rabbits flat on the road after they've been through.

'That's the other thing. He's the size of a rabbit and the

'Not us, eh Flash. I'll tell you what. He's my cobber. He's my little mate. I went down to Balclutha for a few weeks and he pined, he wouldn't eat. He'd die without me.'

shooters would pick him off without knowing. Right Flash?'

Two beady black eyes peered up from ground level.

'I know what's going through your mind Flash. I'd better tie you up before you take off again. Now see this wire? You've got to have that as well as the buckle. He's that smart he can undo the collar . . . away he goes again.

'We had an English couple come into the camp a while back, eh. The man offered me $100 for this dog. He knew how much I'd paid for him. $50 down in Nightcaps when he was five weeks old and no bigger than a rat.

'The next day he was back—$150. Then $200. On the last day he came over with his cheque-book and pen. The final offer: $500!

'Not us, eh Flash. I'll tell you what. He's my cobber. He's my little mate. I went down to Balclutha for a few weeks and he pined, he wouldn't eat. He'd die without me.'

Friday and Flash, McKenzie and Mears. We pulled out and waved to the old man, and I thought—yes. It was part of the same phenomenon.

On across the Mackenzie Country. For the first time we saw heat puddles on the road ahead, and the engine temperature was running eight degrees above normal. This region is an oven which generates the most powerful thermal rise in New Zealand, and the slowly detonating heads of cumulus, rising above brown hills to the east, bore evidence. On across tussock, over blue canals and around Lake Pukaki, the Southern Alps in clear view beyond until . . . *what is that!* A giant hummock rises straight off the plain. On its summit, minute by comparison, is a string of buildings, domes. A monastery?

An observatory. The southern-most professional observatory in the world. I made inquiries at Tekapo and was told to ring.

'Mt John hit us right in the eye. We're travelling the south, if I can explain the method, just picking out things at random.'

'Yes, that's sometimes the best way,' said the voice of the observatory superintendent, Mike Clark; but I had the feeling he was talking about the universe itself.

'Uh huh,' said Clark, as we all watched the key to the camera room go spinning out of his hand and drop down the only grating in sight. 'Murphy's Law.'

But he retrieved it with two long fingers, and the tour began. First, the Harvard sky patrol for which Mt John receives funding from the American university. Cameras are set up to photograph the southern sky in units 30 x 40 degrees. The aim is to build up, over years, a visual history of the stars so that armchair astronomers could compare an identical section of sky with photographs taken perhaps 10 years apart, and pick the stars which are flaring or fading. The big telescopes around the world could then be swung onto a more precise investigation.

'Take a look at this plate.'

The larger stars of the Southern Cross showed up,

familiar enough, but set in a star-field which looked like a blast from an aerosol can.

'The human eye, which is perhaps seven millimetres across, can see stars up to the sixth magnitude, maybe 8000 stars on a clear night. This is taken with a 40 mm lens, and it's a 30-minute exposure so that faint light is collected. But even this . . . every magnitude up the scale brings into view stars two and a half times as faint as the previous limit. The number goes up on an exponential curve, and on the big reflecting telescopes overseas, when you get up to the 21st or 22nd magnitude—it's just a plaster of light.'

The tour moved to the telescopes, the largest of them a 60 cm reflector. Their staple programme is a study of stars locked into a gravitational union. Such binary stars, because of their relative movement one to the other, their occulting and other phenomena, offer the best chance for stellar analysis: real diameter, mass, orbital speeds, composition. The astronomers, muffled against the cold, work there at night with the domes open, for any artificial heat within the building disturbs the viewing quality.

That I wanted to see, but a storm blew up and by nightfall the wind howled. Mt John has many stories of the wind. It can be powerful enough to float stones off the hillside and break windows. The observatory's technician, John Baker, had once been flung 30 metres while trying to secure a dome in a 140-knot gale. Water-tanks had finished up 300 metres down into the lake below.

No one worked that night, but I woke at 4 a.m. and the sky had cleared. I looked out on the stars and tried to imagine what was in fact there. Not just in the Milky Way, which was the galaxy's cross-section, but out in every direction—a plaster of light. The billions of stars of our own galaxy, but beyond that too, the billions of galaxies. I failed and fell asleep.

In the morning, I asked Mike Clark what was the most amazing sight he'd ever seen in the night sky. He went through the options, and the comet he'd discovered 11 years previously was the first to be dismissed.

'Once, in Christchurch, I was going to an astronomical society meeting on my bicycle and the whole landscape started flickering as if it was under a welder's torch. A meteor.

'The Aurora Australis. That's huge of course, by far the biggest visual input . . . .

'But I think neither of those two. It's harder to explain, but I think it's this: to see a super-nova and to know what's going on. The complete annihilation of so much matter. In 1054 our galaxy had a super-nova in the Crab Nebula, and it was a daytime spectacle. Now there are none, but you can watch them in other galaxies. No more than a pin-prick of light, but if you think about it . . . there are billions of stars in that galaxy and the nova is outshining all of them combined. It's awesome.

'A galaxy gets a super-nova once every 100 years on average. You could say we were overdue for our next, and you can hope we're not too close to it. The shock of that energy coming in within our own region would strip the atmosphere right off this planet. But the chances of that are infinitesimal. The super-nova will come. It'll be safely distant, and every telescope in the world will swing onto it. Murphy's Law! You can bet it's going to blow just one degree below the alps over there.'

'We don't believe
in shagpile in the
grandstand'

bruce ansley
photographer: julie riley
16 february 1985

Locals huddle in Kumara's two surviving pubs; tomorrow is race-day but tonight is Friday night and outside the lightning flashes.

On the bar walls in both pubs hangs 'The Kiwi Guide to Life, rule 4: If it moves, bet on it'. The bet is that if it moves at all tomorrow, it will splash.

Pictures of bare-breasted women hang in both bars too, one of them enigmatically on a calendar advertising hydraulic connectors. On the West Coast feminism has its place and it's usually agreed the place is the other side of the Main Divide.

The motor inn in Greymouth serves huge whitebait fritters, scallops, roast lamb and venison.

The Kumara Racing Club's 99th annual race meeting begins on a Ben Hur morning of swirling grey skies. The news on Radio Scenicland is of electrical storms in Auckland and Tauranga. Flood warnings for the West Coast have been out all week, but South Westland has taken the worst. The dark red of the Grey River clashes with the grey Tasman Sea, setting up giant cross-waves. A fishing boat overturned on the bar during the week, drowning the skipper.

The radio commercial for the 99th Kumara races tells of people flocking in from all over the country, even from Australia, for the 'carnival atmosphere of this renowned event'.

The commercial is followed by cancellation notices. Cricket and tennis are postponed. Radio Scenicland offers congratulations to Chief Fire Officer Pat O'Dea, 25 years with the Westport Volunteer Fire Brigade today.

The nor-westerly pushes banks of clouds across the Tasman, hitting the mountains and bouncing tails of spray off the grandstand and stables of the Kumara racecourse, turning the ground into a slime of mud and grass. An old Dennis fire engine stands ready, but it is difficult to light a cigarette. The

Race-day at Kumara is a West Coast institution.

Kiddy Kastle is deflated in the gusts and the popcorn stand hunches, back to the wind. The carnival atmosphere retreats to the bar underneath the corrugated-iron grandstand. Its doors are marked the Sailing Home Bar, the General Gilbert Bar, the Rising Fast Bar and the Phar Lap Bar, but like the slots in the Post Office, most go into the same space.

Bar staff argue over the three television sets inside; officials decree one should be kept on the cricket, two on the races. The corner of the bar in front of the cricket set leaks. No one minds. 'We don't believe in shagpile in the grandstand' says club secretary David Guenole. 'We don't try to be a metropolitan club. People love the old tin-hut style of bar.'

Four men paddle around the car park in white straw hats, their white shoes casualties of the West Coast mud. Aucklanders, the locals agree.

For race three Fred Tibbles, Clerk of the Course, leads the horses around to the back straight. The straight once vanished into the pongas and legends tell of horses and jockeys being switched in there. Locals insist that a mare once vanished into the foliage and after some time emerged at the other end of the straight, foal at foot. In 1936 some smart bookies fetched

On the bar walls in both pubs hangs 'The Kiwi Guide to Life, rule 4: If it moves, bet on it'.

Above: Horses and locals are appropriately shod for the West coast mud.

a big bay down from Auckland and raced it off the limit. Somewhere on the straight it vanished and was not seen on the Coast again; the bookies, it was reported, had got the wind up. Once a trotting race was held directly after a hurdles event and someone forgot about the hurdles on the back straight. Most of the field had to go around them but one horse found a gap, streaked through and won.

In race three this year Bianco Lad breaks free of the barriers, tears right around the track, comes back to the start,

re-starts and wins the race.

In the birdcage after the race Heirport drops dead, to the embarrassment of club officials. Vets open her up on the other side of the road and discover a burst blood vessel. One of the vets remembers a race at Kumara where a horse reared and hit its head at the start. Confusion. The course announcer said the red flag was up and they'd have to stop the race. Everyone in the birdcage ran to the side of the track, waving their hats. The jockeys reined in. Hang on, said the announcer, they've made a mistake. The jockeys spurred their horses and the race was on again.

Fred Tibbles, Clerk of the Course for 35 going on 40 years, has his scarlet coat covered by a red parka. He doesn't seem to mind the slight diminution of glory. He is 76, his horse Tony 24. Tony has been doing the job for 21 years, as well as carrying the Clerk of the Course to the track each race-day.

Tibbles lives in a place no one seems able to pinpoint, waving their arms vaguely to the northwest: 'Over there'. As he pronounces it, it seems likely to be Dunganville, named after Patrick Dungan who found gold in Westland in 1865. On race-days Tony carries Tibbles through No-Name, threading through the bush and over the river to the course. Tibbles is famous for staying in the saddle late on race-days, and for once riding a stag into the bar at the Empire Hotel. (Tibbles says the stag was already in the bar—he just hopped on.)

Kumara saw out the 19th century in frock coat but the old gold town is down to overalls now. Horses in the feature race, the Kumara Gold Nuggets Handicap, still compete for a silver pine box of gold nuggets. Guenole reckons the nuggets put zing into the meeting. They weigh an ounce, less valuable than the $5850 cash prize but more glamorous.

The Kumara Racing Club held its first meeting in 1887, 11 years after gold was discovered at Dillmanstown and the rush was on. The mayor declared the first race-day a public holiday. Ninety-nine meetings on, Kumara has fared better than Dillmanstown next door. Dillmanstown has piles of tailings but Kumara has houses and still appears in the guides as a town.

Hector Sinclair, president of the Kumara Racing Club, was born in Dillmanstown but shifted to Kumara, a move imperceptible to an outsider but quite definite to Coasters. Sinclair, a member of the club for 40 years, became president

Tibbles is famous for staying in the saddle late on race-days, and for once riding a stag into the bar at the Empire Hotel.

when Bill Stewart died five years ago after 38 years in office. Sinclair's nephew Hamish is vice-president; family links tie the stewards together. 'It's not acually a family affair,' says the elder Sinclair. 'It's just who you can get to help.'

Lightning crackles over Greymouth. The electrical storm cuts the power to Kumara. Only the tote continues to operate, on batteries. Should they call it off, ponders a race official, or carry on with no race-caller or anything, just like the old days? They carry on, officials anxiously pointing out that this storm is Greymouth's, and nothing to do with them.

On-course betting is well down on last year although Guenole boasts that Kumara invariably tops on-course turnover on the West Coast circuit. And it is better than in 1892, when Mr Kennedy's Ohaura beat Dr McBrearty's Miss Lacey in the Produce Stakes. Only a pound was invested on the tote, on Ohaura. It was duly returned.

About 2600 people pass through the gates this year, half the usual number. By the last race the rain is determined, sweeping into the first few rows of the old stand and forcing everyone to the back in a cluster of glistening, steaming humanity.

The meeting is thoroughly sodden at its end but only club officials are downcast. People head for the bars in town.

The Empire and the Theatre Royal are full of noise and laughter. Late in the evening the police arrive but there is no urban animosity towards the two constables, nor any hostility from them. The crowd joke with them; someone takes a constable's cap and wears it until he leaves.

Next day the mud is thick with tote tickets and rubbish. The club decides to leave cleaning it up until it dries out. The DB tanker outside the bar is still awash internally, and bogged in the wet ground.

One of the 99-year-old frosted windows in the ancient white-painted officials' building is broken. A jagged hole punctures the neat black lettering announcing that this is the secretary's office. Someone put an elbow through it, says Sinclair.

He mourns the fine summer nights, the people spilling out of the pub, onto the main street on race-day. 'It was a disaster, really,' he said of the 99th annual race meeting.

In the mid-1970s the Kumara Racing Club was threatened with official extinction. It survived and is planning its centenary next year. 'There's always room for a small country club,' says Sinclair. 'That's why people come here. Riccarton and places like that, it's sort of a business. We seem to have something the rest of the country hasn't got.'

In the main street of Kumara a house is for sale, marked down from $15,000 to $12,000. In the township of Ngahere Father Paddy Thwaites, parish priest, is pondering the performance of his horse De Porres in the last race. Beside the stables the open-air gents with the lichen-covered two by fours holding up its corrugated iron walls stands empty as the last Commodore vanishes up the road.

Te Riri Ture

bruce ansley

photographer: jane ussher

21 september 1985

'The anger of the law' has been used for over 100 years to separate the Maori from their land. East Coast land rights claimants are now challenging that law and asking the Crown to return land they have always considered theirs.

When Judge John Hole, who had pointed features and straight fair hair and was indisputably Pakeha, told Hamana Keelan and Sue Nikora and Jill Kaa their letter from the Minister offered little hope for their land claim they were only mildly indignant.

Judge Hole, you see, handled the whole affair pretty well. When the young defendants from Ruatoria came into his Gisborne courtroom, with their old jeans and dreadlocks and bravado, and called rastafarian slogans to one another, he let them be. He let them put their bucket of orange drink on the bench and stick rasta signs on the microphone stand and go home at night on the strength of their word to return the next day. All he asked in return was that they allow his court to conduct its business as well as might be and keep their playing cards in their pockets.

But the judge was Pakeha despite all that. Whereas Koro Wetere, the Minister of Maori Affairs, was Maori. When Judge Hole looked at Wetere's letter and told Keelan and Nikora and Kaa it did not mean they were getting back 1.12 million hectares of claimed tribal lands, the three took it equably enough. Wetere was Maori writing to Maori. A Pakeha might think he was saying 18 of their 20 separate claims had been rejected and the remaining two cautiously admitted, but a Maori would know he was in fact saying the very opposite, that 18 were accepted and two needed a little more work.

After all, their claims were fair, merely what the Treaty of Waitangi promised them, and Koro, they recalled, had said as much to them on the marae, a court as high as any of the Pakeha's. Later, in the small living room with crisp white antimacassars on the royal-red chairs, and ornate furniture and careful photographs, the lines of Keelan's face grew severe. 'The interpretation of anyone saying that letter is bad news doesn't know how to read,' he said. 'That's good news.'

There is a phrase, *te riri ture*, 'the anger of the law'. The young rastafarians were incurring it now, although perhaps not in its accepted sense. They were in Judge Hole's courtroom because they had allegedly encamped on someone else's property and one thing led to another. Keelan, Nikora and Kaa were in court as driving members of the Ngati Porou/Mt Hikurangi Land Claims Committee. As a human rights group they were protecting the rastas' rights. As a land rights group they were arguing that the defendants were on ancestral land which Wetere was now returning to them, so where was the trespass?

The Gisborne courthouse is a modern concrete-and-glass affair near the Turanganui River, still slimy from recent floods. The lobby is not unused to wild scenes; in the old days the Black Power and Mongrel Mob fought here, hurling furniture down the stairs. Today there was nothing more lethal than a ghetto-blaster which a constable wanted off: 'This is a *courtroom*!'

The amazing thing about this case was the escalation factor. Some young people had been causing a lot of upset in Ruatoria. A few had been disowned by relatives, told to leave home. The rastafarians *looked* dangerous too. Tales of mayhem circulated. A story appeared in the *Gisborne Herald* headlined 'Ruatoria, a Town of Fear'. It was a statement by a local National Party official.

With all these curious looking coves about, waving their bibles and talking of someone called Jah and spouting a nihilistic vision in which goods and chattels had no place, some people walked a little faster and locked up at night. So when Chris Campbell moved into an old house on a block at Whareponga with his wife, and Hone Heeney and Dick Maxwell and a lot of others followed them in, Keita Walker, chairperson of the Maori incorporation running the station, and her husband George, who managed the farm, were disposed to get them off again—even if three of the kids were her nephews.

Besides, many were related on the coast. The constable who first warned the group off the land was Campbell's brother. One of the defendants was Keelan's son, one of the prosecution witnesses Heeney's mother.

In Gisborne Inspector Mick Huggard, founder member of the armed offenders squad, was not about to take the matter lightly. There had been complaints of burglary, theft from cars and criminal damage.

In the end none of the rastas was charged with burglary, theft or criminal damage but it was a time for taking no chances. Inspector Huggard rounded up a posse of 40 policemen, including 18 members of the armed offenders

The account of the ensuing drama lay somewhere between *Spartacus* and *Ghostbusters*.

squad, dogs and a helicopter, and the whole outfit burst upon the rastas around dawn on June 11.

The account of the ensuing drama lay somewhere between *Spartacus* and *Ghostbusters*. Some stayed where they were. Some fled on horseback and were rounded up by helicopter. Some were picked up later. They all appeared in court on so many charges everyone lost count but after some had been added and some dropped it came out to 163. This was the scene Judge Hole surveyed through his glasses, like Wellington after Waterloo.

Huggard knew the stories about people on the coast keeping weapons in their utes, loaded shotguns beside their beds at night. He could only advise against guns. People held meetings to sort things out. The rastas pulled down 10 km of fences on Taitai station one day, had the matter out on the marae and spent half a day putting them back up again. Three haybarns were burned down in what Campbell called a land protest: 'I was in clink. But if I'd been out might have held the match myself.'

Curiously, two of the haybarns were on Colin Williams's property. Wetere has undertaken to buy Williams's Pakahiroa station as part of his plan for giving the symbolic Mt Hikurangi back to the Ngati Porou.

None of this was really needed by the Ngati Porou/Mt Hiku-rangi land claims committee, members of Te Aitanga a Mate subtribe, whose vast claim did not, in any event, enjoy universal support. In some places on the coast, talk of the land claim is met with a deep and ominous silence. The rastas are an added embarrassment.

The evening sessions with the land claims committee always began and ended with a prayer in Maori. I stood uncomfortably while the soft sounds filled the room. The effect was hypnotic, a mourning for turangawaewae, for self-esteem inseparable from the land.

We talked about the land claim, a breathtaking affair stretching from Tikirau, Cape Runaway in the north along the Raukumara Ranges to Mohaka in the south, 1.12 m hectares of land with Mt Hikurangi as the centrepiece and the economic zone out to sea added, along with rights to forests, hunting, water and fisheries. They wanted every square metre back, with compensation for its use; all of it, they said, could be traced back to a common ancestor whose descendants never lost their sovereignty: 'We never gave it away willingly. Our lands have been mismanaged, misadministered and wrongly confiscated by the Crown against the principles, spirit and covenants of Articles 2 and 3 of the Treaty of Waitangi.' For their claim encompassed some 600,000 hectares which they said was first confiscated after the Te Kooti uprising, in which the Ngati Porou were the Crown's

Kupenga's headless body was later discovered in a hole; one of the group in court was charged with his murder.

allies, and further alienated under a series of statutes, culminating in the Maori Affairs Amendment Act 1967.

They talked with total confidence. They were *right*. The treaty said the land was theirs and the treaty was a legal and binding contract between partners. They had never disposed of their land. If it was someone else's, where was the proof? There was none. The land claim was an act of faith. I pulled documents from my briefcase, legal articles, opinions, reports, and their faces tightened. Their 20 years of research had not been from a Pakeha point of view, but from that of the Maori: 'We rely on the strength and power of it.'

Midway, Nikora held up a hand to talk of something else. Lance Kupenga had disappeared and she had put up his bail. They were not supporting anyone who broke the law. He must be fetched back. Kupenga's headless body was later discovered in a hole; one of the group in court was charged with his murder. At the close of that evening there was another small service. Hamiona Keelan, one of the rasta group, read from the Book of John: 'Love not the world, neither the things *that are* in the world . . .'

The Ngati Awa of Whakatane function amid less drama. On March 2, 1865, the Rev Carl Volkner was hanged from a tree outside his church at Opotiki. On July 21 of that year James Te Mautaranui Fulloon was killed at Whakatane.

He had broken a line of tapu established to keep out the Pakeha and Te Arawa. The 1928 Sim Commission on confiscated native lands and other grievances found that the murders were not in themselves acts of rebellion and 'if the natives of Opotiki and Whakatane had not resisted the armed forces sent to capture the murderers there would not have been any excuse for confiscating their lands'. The settler-dominated, land-hungry government needed little excuse and as Keith Sinclair noted, it enjoyed a good deal of popularity: '. . . all were keen to defend the honour of the Crown, to fight for the liberty of the individual Maori to sell his land and to get some of it'.

The Ngati Awa argued that Fulloon's killing could have been treated as a simple law and order matter requiring only a police action. Instead, the government sent in the troops. The Ngati Awa resisted: 'The military force came to subdue the very mana and tapu that the tribe was trying to uphold.' Because they resisted they fell within the embrace of the invidious New Zealand Settlements Act 1863 and amendments, which allowed the government to punish unruly Maori by confiscating their lands—which, of course, could then be made available to settlers.

The Ngati Awa were devastated and Maori customary law, too, suffered a further defeat. Some 46,500 ha were finally confiscated. Thirty-five Ngati Awa chiefs and warriors were captured and after a bogus court-martial sent to Auckland for trial.

Five were executed, three died in prison. The Treaty of Waitangi, affording the Maori the full, exclusive and undisturbed possession of their lands, and extending the tribes the royal protection, suffered too. But the New Zealand Settlements Act had already trammelled the treaty. It was not long before the courts held that legally it was of no consequence.

In the case of Wi Parata v the Bishop of Wellington in 1877 the politician-turned-judge, Chief Justice Sir James Prendergast, declared the treaty to be 'a simple nullity'. The Privy Council in a subsequent case said Prendergast had gone too far; nevertheless, the courts have since held that the treaty was not legally binding and would remain invalid until incorporated in New Zealand law. This, successive governments have declined to do. They did, however, pass successive acts of Parliament, effectively greasing the machinery for separating the Maori from their land.

With the courts closed to them the Ngati Awa appealed to the Crown, as represented by the government. 'Our case,' said Professor Sid Mead, the tribe's chief negotiator, 'is based on our belief that what the government did to us is *unconstitutional*. We signed the Treaty of Waitangi and the treaty was supposed to have *protected* us. The irony of it is that *we* were attacked by the British—and it was the British who were supposed to have guaranteed our safety.

'It has been said they did what they did because the government had no legal obligations under the treaty. We will *never* accept that. It is an egocentric, ego-British way of looking at it. I don't think we can go on accepting that the treaty is nothing. The Pakeha has done quite well accepting that position. My people have not done so well.'

The Ngati Awa are claiming $11.6m in compensation for the 46,500 ha of confiscated land and for human suffering. They want the 1197 ha of farm and forestry land administered by the Crown, the Ngati Awa block, returned to them. They want four reserves near Whakatane totalling 885.3 ha to be rezoned Maori reserves.

Two hapu of the Ngati Awa, the Ngati Rangihouri and Ngati Hikakino, petitioned Parliament for the return of some of their land after the confiscations. The Sim Commission, which found the confiscations in the Bay of Plenty to be 'fair and just' (despite its conclusion that some land may have been confiscated without compensation from loyal sub-tribes), recommended some land be given to the two hapu.

That recommendation has gently dragged on through reams of bureaucrats' letters ever since. Nothing was done. The Ngati Awa say it is now time for the Crown to pay up, and

Children at Ruatoria township.

suggest a Lands and Survey administered farm at Kawerau be given in settlement. A later matter to be resolved is the return of Mt Edgecumbe, near Kawerau.

They want a full pardon for the chiefs and men taken and tried in 1865. They want legislation to establish the Ngati Awa Trust Board as a tribal trust and enough money to set it up as an administrative authority for tribal affairs, including the returned lands. And they seek the return of the meeting house, Mataatua, carved by Ngati Awa chiefs in the 1870s and given to the Queen in the hope the gift would encourage the Crown to return the tribe's confiscated lands. The house is now in the Otago Museum.

The National Government in 1983 offered a final settlement of up to $320,000 in value. The Ngati Awa, recognising it to be a once-and-for-all claim, then widened its case and resubmitted it. The Labour Government inherited the claim.

The tribe, however, does not anticipate an easier path now: 'People take this government to be very sympathetic,' said Mead, 'but when it comes down to brass tacks it is the same, very hard-nose. The National administration was the first government *ever* to admit there was a case, that there *was* a grievance to be settled. Now we're arguing over the arithmetic.'

Chief Judge Ed Durie and the Waitangi Tribunal had been treading a fine line between what was acceptable to their Maori supplicants on one side and the Government on the other. In their decision on the despoilation of the Manukau Harbour and the loss of surrounding lands to the Manukau tribes, their biggest claim to date, they took a deeper breath and longer stride.

The tribunal's decision accommodated the Maori magico-religious view of the environment and conservation, encompassing sea gods and guardian spirits and arrangements generally foreign to the due workings of the law. It paid homage to Maori values and opened the door to an abiding sense of outrage. It found that a metaphysical concern was relevant to the Treaty of Waitangi, found that the Maori interest in waters and the foreshore accorded them by the treaty could no longer be denied, tilted at the prosaic, departmental approach and attitudes to Maoritanga.

The Treaty of Waitangi Act set out to give the treaty some practical effect, admittedly by a rather indirect route; it could sidestep damning legal precedent and to a degree reinstate Maori customary law swept aside in the inrush of pragmatic Pakeha law. The tribunal functioned to overturn Prendergast's rejection of the treaty as a simple nullity. And land claims will come increasingly into its purview.

Te riri ture, the anger of the law. It brought Pukaki within a breath of annihilation. The Pukaki village appears in the Sim Commission report, which approved of Sir John Gorst's account; Pukaki was inhabited by relations of the Waikato tribes. A large proportion of its people were old and infirm, yet 'the instant war broke out we found it dangerous, though we had 10,000 men in the field, to allow these poor creatures to remain in their homes. They were driven out, their property looted and destroyed, and their land confiscated.'

The people were left with little more than 60 ha; even their burial ground was confiscated (still used, although partly dug up by a stock car track in the 1970s). The land dwindled: the adjacent Auckland airport restricted development, people moved away in despair.

Eventually only 3 ha of the original Pukaki lands remained as Maori lands—and, people believed, a little over 1 ha set aside for the marae. But by a series of blunders in which two orders of the Maori Land Court were not acted upon, the marae and access roadway were accidentally sold along with most of the land by a court-appointed trustee.

Today nothing remains of the Pukaki marae that supported some 200 families in the 1950s, apart from three houses on the remaining pockets of Maori land.

'Pukaki,' declared the tribunal, 'illustrates the way in which Maori people have lost their lands, homes, sacred places and fisheries through insensitive and (to them) incomprehensible laws and regulations. Today nothing remains of the Pukaki marae that supported some 200 families in the 1950s, apart from three houses on the remaining pockets of Maori land.'

The tribunal's recommendations concerning the Manukau claim are now before the Government; they include a proposal to buy back the Pukaki marae site and lagoon and set them aside as Maori reserves.

But the tribunal also urged the Government to go beyond its recommendations, to consider those hurts which were still outside the tribunal's jurisdiction.

It was, it said, appalled at the events of the past, and although it was referring to the Manukau, its abhorrence will undoubtedly extend to other areas.

An amendment to the act will extend the tribunal's jurisdiction back beyond the present limit, 1975, to 1840, exposing that 'enormous sense of grievance, injustice and outrage' that has been nurtured for more than a century . . .

loosing it at considerable cost to the taxpayer, as pointed out by Winston Peters, the Opposition's Maori Affairs spokesperson, during the second reading of the bill.

The tribunal has worked through some 22 claims of various kinds; seven are still awaiting a hearing. The Government has before it a string of claims ranging from the aftermath of the Raglan golf course affair to the Hauraki goldfields to the Wanganui river bed. The Treaty of Waitangi hui in February this year raised many more (including eight from the Department of Maori Affairs).

The Government is still considering the Ngati Porou claims, although Wetere has undertaken to return Mt Hikurangi and has indicated that two claims involving small areas at Mohaka and Awapuni lagoon have some substance.

(The Prime Minister, David Lange, has written to Keelan saying that while the return of Hikurangi mountain and other disputed lands to Ngati Porou was being carefully considered, he understood from Wetere no land had ever been confiscated from the tribe for any reason.)

The Government is still contemplating the Ngati Awa claim and there are signs of embarrassment over the delay in giving an answer.

The giant claims from the Taranaki and Waikato confiscations are still waiting in the wings. Perhaps they will go before the reconstituted Waitangi Tribunal, perhaps their mana will demand they go directly to the Crown. (Where the tribunal's recommendations go in any event; government departments are effectively the tribunal's appeal authorities, since *they* decide what action will be taken.)

There is a clear warning in the tribunal's Manukau decision, however, that compromise will be necessary, that some land cannot be returned: 'In many cases, compensation is the only practical option today.' Some wounds may never heal.

Golden Bay— End of the Rainbow

bruce ansley

photographer: bruce foster

5 november 1988

The closing of the cement works was a big blow for the small community of Golden Bay—but it takes more than the collapse of a major industry to depress a place close to paradise.

All day they've been decorating the concrete block hall with the manorial signature of the Golden Bay Cement Company over the door. Nearby are the Golden Bay Cement Company's tennis courts. These boys really looked after their workers until quite recently. Winstone, owned by Brierley Investments, bought the company in May last year. Fletcher Challenge bought half from Brierley last September, and the two giants, right there in the vanguard of the new-look New Zealand, ran the company together until March when Fletcher took the lot.

Four months later Fletcher announced that the Tarakohe works, 80 years working around the clock, would close. Deregulation of the industry meant cheaper imports. Domestic demand was falling. Cement workers wondered what the country was coming to when you couldn't sell concrete to New Zealanders. Then Finance Minister Roger Douglas talked on television about the township of Tarakohe. The cement workers wondered what the Government was coming to, also. Where'd he been? Not at Tarakohe; there's no township, only the cement works.

The Golden Bay Cement Company's Tarakohe factory may be the most scenic cement works in the world. It sits beside a small harbour. To its left are the long, glorious beaches of Golden Bay. On the right the bay's pale sand gives way to the gold of Tasman Bay in bush-fringed coves stretching around to Kaiteriteri.

The road winds past the cement works, under a massive limestone outcrop, through a hole in the rock around the Wainui Inlet and over to Totaranui in the Abel Tasman National Park.

It is close to paradise, although perspectives can differ, as they do with Dave Amos, deputy manager, 23 years at the plant and with a weary manner not wholly because of the flu he's suffering from. He's taking early retirement— right here. Well, even on the West Coast you can move from Westport to Hokitika. In Golden Bay you can go from Takaka 27 km down the track to Collingwood. Cell-block C, says Amos.

That night everyone from the works, past and present, goes to the do in the hall. The band is playing ('knock, knock, knocking on heaven's door') and they dance the foxtrot beneath silver foil and huge paper butterflies stuck on the walls. Tomorrow 85 more people will be out of work and the last 45 will wind down the plant.

If Hugh Fletcher happened by no one would spit on him. They're moderate by city standards. That afternoon a group of half a dozen couldn't remember the last time they'd been on strike: 51? No, that was a lockout. Maybe two days a few years back, in support of drivers.

They're more intent tonight on using up the social club funds. The company has promised to pick up anything extra and they're determined there'll be something to pay. There's resentment but no real malice. After all, says Gary Jacob, it's true what they say in the papers: an optimist is someone who brings their lunch to work.

No other place is quite like Golden Bay. The road in, over the Takaka Hill, is legendary. They say you can do it in half an hour. In fact, Constable Tony Cunningham knows you can because once he was calling for help as he chased an escaped prisoner and the cavalry came over from Motueka in 30 minutes; but the traffic sergeant in the back jumped out and stowed his sick bag under a bush.

Most take a little longer. In the motorists' legend the Takaka hill ranks with the Otira. Every summer there's a trail of steaming, expired machinery all the way to the top. The road runs through little peaks of grey marble along the top then drops through four mighty zigs and zags into the green of Golden Bay.

It is the only way in or out, unless you walk to the West Coast by way of the Heaphy Track, for the Tasman Mountains fence off the bay to the south. Some 70 km of highway lead through the bay with perhaps 300 km of lesser roads, no more than you'd get in a middling suburb.

Four thousand six hundred and forty-seven people live in this whole top left-hand corner of the South Island. The other curious thing about that statistic is that it conceals a large number of Germans. Folklore in the bay is that 10 percent of the population is German. Some say more, some less. The 1986 Census showed only 180 German and Austrian-born people living in the wider Nelson statistical district but the big influx was post-Chernobyl; that is, post-census.

At the end of the road skirting Wainui Inlet, running over a one-way wooden bridge and through unbelievably green farmland, you come to the Tui community, where Reinhardt found the end of the rainbow. When Reinhardt came here his surname was Fuchs. Now it is Kanuka. He looks a little like Jesus Christ, with thinning hair. His voice is as gently soporific as Horlicks. Kanuka had tried to set up a community near Nelson but neighbouring farmers objected and, Kanuka says

charitably, they were right: 'It was not the place.'

Golden Bay *was* the place. No pollution, no nearby farmers with sprays, beaches which in Europe would have rich people keeping out the rest: 'In Germany the rivers, the trees are not dying, they're dead. I lived in a beautiful place, a water mill, and they built a nuclear power station next to it.'

Besides, Golden Bay County was the first in the country to plan for communities—no small factor when you consider, for example, the tough time the Buller County Council, on the other side of the range, gave alternative life-stylers when they first moved in: some county officers saw them as part of a world-wide hippie conspiracy.

Kanuka, once an architect, bought the farm and planned a village where people could do as they pleased. His own house is built around a rock which absorbs heat and releases it into the house. It is finished with linseed oil and beeswax and smells of incense.

His roof delighted building inspector (and acting county clerk) Noel Riley. Its shingles, laid by a German craftsperson, are curved into flashings. Riley went along to the housewarming party.

I'd given Kanuka's wife, Jutta, a ride the day before. She'd been hitch-hiking with three of the community's children. She spoke with a German accent, but the kids' voices were 24-carat Kiwi. Some children go to Motupipi school, others don't go to school, leading to friction with the authorities: 'It's their choice.' Everything here is choice. Kanuka goes to men's groups. 'Some farmers come, people who once I would not risk to touch.' A new chapter of progress in the paddocks.

We said goodbye. He stroked my back, placed his hand over his heart, and off I went, past the shingled octagonal house, past the long narrow houses being built on the ridge, past the khaki bus with 'uppity women unite' on it and the house-truck with the

trying to revive the carcase.

The miners were here early—the first payable gold in the South Island was discovered at Lightbands Gully in 1856—and the millers felled the bush. The farmers held on, as they always did. People such as the Harwoods, Hopes and Stranges were the stayers. Others dug in and clung to a lifestyle that seemed meagre by the standards of more affluent areas. Isolation, the small population, breed a tenacity of mind.

People with tenure, like old-stagers everywhere, look at newcomers with suspicion, and these were some newcomers: they were mostly young, dressed differently, spoke in strange accents, built wonderful and curious houses among the weatherboards and gables.

Tensions flourish in such a place. The gold-miners in the hills co-existed quite peacefully until the pickings got slim and they became competitors. The cement workers complain they're just rubbishy concrete workers to the rest of the place and the town grizzles that the cement workers are overpaid and anyway go over the hill to shop.

The dope growers exist in their own penumbra of paranoia; when you don't know who you can trust and who's a narc the safest thing to do is stick with a few people you know well. As quite a lot of marijuana is grown in Golden Bay, and the police devote a great deal of effort to finding it, the growers (who, incidentally, complain that their problems are essentially the same as any other primary producer, except that marketing is even more difficult) become both cunning and insular.

Naturally, the non-growers have more than a passing interest in the identity of the growers, and speculation flourishes like weeds in the damp. Matthew and Ruth Benge, for example, are developing the biggest kiwifruit and nashi growing industry in the southern hemisphere, just outside Takaka. They were not happy to find themselves the targets of rumours.

big bay window, past the breast-shaped kiln and the shed for craftspeople and the dunny brightly painted with flowers, past the old homestead where the community was having lunch, past the old Holdens and Falcons in the car park and out to my Hertz Mitsubishi Mirage with the Cyclone engine, feeling corrupt.

Golden Bay, area 266,250 ha, 61 per cent Crown land, 11 per cent owned, until quite recently when the block was split up and sold, by the Baigent family. Only 23 per cent of the place is good for farming; the rest is marble or mountain, or pakihi, for this place has a West Coast, warm, high-rainfall climate. At its narrowest point you can drive from Pakawau near Cape Farewell and be on the West Coast at Whanganui Inlet, one of the superb, unknown places in this country, in a few minutes.

In parts the bay has that stripped-out, ripped-out feeling you get in such regions as the West Coast, the East Coast or the Coromandel, where people have cut down or dug up everything there is to be had and are left amid the remains,

In fact, the Benges still suffer under a residual suspicion of newcomers. Unbiased animosity comes their way; from conservatives because they're progressive, from the city refugees because of their big business methods and their sprays, from bureaucracy because they're there: once the bureaucrats ordered them to move a shelter belt 15cm.

Constable Cunningham, Golden Bay's sole police officer and a huge, friendly man, keeps an eye on possibly troublesome feuding. For example, Peter Butler and two associates have a mining claim up the Anatoki River. The access road runs through the Rainbow community but it's private and the community doesn't want the miners there. The paper (legal) road, however, runs through the community's buildings. Will the miners take to the bulldozers? Cunningham hopes not. Meanwhile the county council is trying to sort out the argument.

Other disputes take stranger forms. One character, smarting under a slight, saved animal offal for weeks and, last New Year's Eve, dumped the whole stinking, crawling mess on his victim's verandah. 'What can I say?' said the judge, and fined him the maximum.

Cunningham's life is mainly peaceful despite the faintly bizarre nature of the place, extending even into the dull grey of local politics.

While the rest of the country was mucking about with roading and drainage in the last local body elections, Golden Bay was enmeshed in unique issues. The county council was then average: two women, the rest middle-aged men. Two election issues set the place afire. A private museum was one: radicals wanted the council to buy it, conservatives did not. Inasmuch as it is possible to become heated over artefacts, the argument smoked along.

More compelling was the question of the hedge along the property of some new-breed locals. The council thought it was

The town was thoroughly divided when . . . county clerk Warwick Bennett nipped out . . . cut down the hedge himself.

untidy. They wanted it cut down. The owners and their supporters did not. A save-our-hedge campaign gathered sound and fury. The council debated the hedge four times and when the works foreman and his gang turned up with their chainsaws there were the opposition lined up, ready to trade their limbs for the hedges.

The town was thoroughly divided when, early one Saturday morning, county clerk Warwick Bennett nipped out and, while everyone was still asleep, cut down the hedge himself.

Uproar! The old council was largely turfed out in the election. Now its chairperson is a woman, Ann Lewis. Half the councillors are women. The council is younger, more innovative—at least, when they got into their stride, for at first time was taken up arguing over whether there should be chocolate biscuits for morning tea, while the ratepayers were out there struggling. Councillors now face towards the public instead of away from them. The old photos of the Queen have gone, replaced by a plain grey wall with a white workboard. And a new hedge was planted at No 9, Waitapu Rd, complete with tree-planting ceremony.

Before he left for a new job in Opunake Bennett was interviewed by *Motueka-Golden Bay News* reporter Carol Dawber. Completely unrepentant, the dawn raider railed at the 'house cow spinning wheel people . . . suckers, hanging on'.

Over in Puponga, Oscar Climo sits in a house 22 km from where he'd been born, a small house his family grew up in. Before the war Climo spent three years in the scow *Portland*, sailing between Puponga and Nelson. He left for the war and was torpedoed five times. Once he spent 23 days in a lifeboat, was rescued by a Dutch tanker off South America, was torpedoed again the following morning and back into a lifeboat. He met his wife Betty in London during the war and told her of the bustling place he'd take her home to. When he left, Puponga had a working mine, dancehall, bakehouse. The Climos returned to a ghost town. Everything was shut, even the shop.

But they stayed in this enchanting corner of the country and Betty came to love it as much as Oscar. One by one his brothers are coming home to live, three of them now, looking out over the tidal flats and the remains of the wharf, over the small peninsula which was once an island and fortified pa. Te Rauparaha wiped out many of the local Maori; once they found a woman's skeleton on the beach, skull cleft by an axe blow.

The old people go and younger ones replace them and the Climos in their oasis of peace take things as they come, even the police helicopters flying over a couple of times a year with the drug squad. Climo sips his malt whisky in the living room, in the collection of small houses that make up the northernmost civilisation in the South Island. 'Leave? Where is there to go?'

Some hoped the huge influx of money from the cement company's severance cheques would lead to an outbreak of entrepreneurial vigour in Golden Bay. Some of the cheques were large. On the last day of September most workers walked out of the gates. At the top end they carried away six-figure sums. Someone with 30 years' service picked up 62 weeks' redundancy pay (the average yearly pay was more than $30,000) plus superannuation. A lot of people had been at the works a long time: the average age of the work-force was 42, and a quarter were in the 54–60 age range.

But there's a natural reluctance to risk life savings. A few bought existing businesses. Fletcher Challenge set up a task force to help workers find other jobs but it was little used. Most don't want to leave the bay. Some are moving to Australia and others are thinking about it ('the newspapers have sits vac columns *that thick*'). Others are sitting tight to see what might develop.

The bay is resigned to the loss of its major industry; in fact, by the time you reach Collingwood you'd never know it was a calamity at all. The cement workers tend to be bitter, regarding themselves as the latest victims of a politico-business conspiracy. Says Gary Jacob: 'They think we're fools, but we're not. We know what's going on but we just can't do anything about it—there's no one to kick.'

So far no one has rushed in to bag the cement company's site, although the nearby yacht club wants to use the office building beside the harbour.

Yet this is a place for enterprise. It has one of the most crowded crafts trails in the country. The work centre in Takaka is a warren of small, craft industry. The local abattoir went broke but has been revived by a consortium of farmers. The Benges grow their kiwifruit and nashis, look forward to employing up to 200 people and talk of expanding into California. In the mountains bands of goldminers poach claims, wading through rivers in their wet suits, lugging suction pumps and riffle boxes. There's even a new picture theatre in town.

Once, in Totaranui, an American looked over the Christmas crowd lying on the golden sand or swimming in the clear water. 'It's very beautiful,' he said, 'but what do you *do* here?' It seems an attractive enough dilemma.

The Wonders of
Waipukurau

b r u c e   a n s l e y
photographer: helena hughes
17 june 1989

Twenty years ago the biggest attraction in Waipukurau was the stock sales. Now the town boasts a three-week arts festival, and the local police sergeant is attracting a lot of attention nationally with his novel method of keeping down crime.

The night the drought breaks in Waipukurau it looks, for a moment, as if everyone might tear off their clothes and spring naked into the rain. The first juicy splats on the tin roof stop the debate in the cattle rostrum. Someone calls for five minutes' silence but there's too much hooray for most to hear. As the rain settles in and the saleyards turn to mud and the air becomes cold and damp it is clear that this is going to be a great night.

It's also plain that things have changed in Waipukurau, aside from the fanciful notion of the citizenry leaping around under a shower of discarded hand-knits. Here we are in the cattle rostrum, whose beautiful worn timbers and vaulted ceilings have the look of a chapel. It was a certified holy place when I was a reporter here covering the stock sales 20 years ago. Farmers robed in Harris tweed, muttered incantations at the procession of beasts below. It's a little like that tonight actually, with the rostrum turned into a debating chamber and six city folks strutting their stuff.

No buyers on the benches tonight, but every one is packed with celebrants sinking white wine and DB, for this is the end of the town's third arts festival. If there are outraged cockies in the house thinking sacrilege they're keeping quiet about it. Waipukurau and arts festivals would have mixed uneasily once. There's a story in how this one got going.

Waipukurau is a farming town, and a farmer's one. It is too far away from the coast for a sniff of the sea, not close enough to the Ruahines for the mountains to have inspired much more than the occasional sign on a gate, Bel Vista or Mountainvue. But the district is fertile. The land is good, settled and rich— or was, once. You could drive over the Pukeora hill and look at the valley through a wooden archway bidding you welcome. The whole works was spread out below you, capital of Central Hawke's Bay, once arguably the nation's richest farming area, full of arrogance and money and the illusion of power. Brown and burned this summer, usually its green grass and English trees covered a million small snobberies expressed in accents that could shatter a railways cup.

Farmers took themselves seriously here. They dressed in brown and sat around horseshoe-shaped tables for monthly council meetings. They were the backbone of the nation, the natural leaders. They supported a cabinet minister (Duncan MacIntyre) and a Speaker (Sir Richard Harrison). Once, at a meeting of the Patangata County Council (there were three counties, a borough, an electric power board, a catchment board and any number of committees to keep a public-spirited citizen busy), a councillor described his indignation during a recent trip to Wellington. The townies drove *one to a car*. Farmers made the money, he declared, and the others squandered it. All around the table heads bobbed sorrowfully.

The farmers liked sending their children to boarding schools out of the district, not so much for a better education (which was not highly regarded) but as a mark of distinction. The high point of the year was the A and P Show, allegedly a meeting place for town and country, but in fact an arena where both sides could judge the gap between them.

You can stand, this weekend, at the top of the Pukeora hill and see the drought. The droughts of North Otago and South Canterbury evolved, so that you could watch the ewes getting thinner and the farmers more desperate bulletin by bulletin. This one just happened. It simply stopped raining in September and one day the district realised this was a fully paid-up disaster.

Like farmers in other drought regions they were already in poor shape to handle a calamity. Even old-money farmers found themselves in trouble. In a countryside dotted with the big old houses of the landed this was like seeing the archbishop at the STD clinic—titillating, but deeply worrying.

Some of the old guard have sold up. Others are surviving; some have thrived, buying more farmland cheaply. The cards are in the air. But the esprit de corps stays true.

The idea came from England, not surprisingly, in a place whose manners are often cribbed from half a world away. Tom Atchison, farmer, gathered kindred spirits around him.

The idea became Grasshoppers, a group of very important men who would invite other men of comparable status to give them the inside running on the way the country was going. They were the natural leaders, after all. For their part the Grasshoppers would observe Chatham rules; they would keep mum.

In a countryside dotted with the big old houses of the landed this was like seeing the archbishop at the STD clinic—titillating, but deeply worrying.

So Roger Douglas came along and told them what was really happening to the economy (in the days when, as Minister of Finance, he might have been expected to know). They didn't believe him, of course. Moreover, Douglas's press secretary, unaware of the confidential nature of the Grasshoppers' undertaking, included the meeting in the minister's weekly list of engagements.

Diana Marriott, a reporter for the Hawke's Bay *Herald-Tribune*, was sent to cover Douglas's speech to the Grasshoppers. The venue was Waipukurau's gentlemen's club, men only. She was allowed to take the great man's photograph and receive his speech notes, and was ushered from the premises.

Well, was this bunch of self-important old blokes to have matters all their own way? Marriott, who is also a district councillor, thought not. What eats grasshoppers? was the call among her friends. Wetas. They formed Weta. But what were they to do? They came up with the very good idea of fostering the arts in Central Hawke's Bay. Weta came to stand for We Appreciate The Arts. A three-week arts festival has been held for the past three years. Norsewear, the knitwear firm in Norsewood, now puts up $6000 in prizes.

In another way the town has arrived. Waipukurau once had a Chamber of Commerce whose chairman was usually manager of one of the town's banks, leaving as soon as his transfer came through. At meetings they would sit around a table in wooden chairs upholstered in green, looking solemn. They'd talk about giving the town a shot in the arm. The metaphor was fair enough because most of the schemes they dreamed up would have calcified the veins of a far more vibrant creature than poor Waipukurau.

They plotted a casino and a jumbo jet airport which would bring planeloads of bewildered tourists to wander these sylvan, well-stocked fields. They imagined industrialists' eyes alight with the pure fire of discovery if only they could be persuaded to recognise the true potential of the town, whose only heavy industry at the time, apart from local bodies, was the Peter Pan ice cream factory.

Peter Pan has nipped off somewhere else now but Waipukurau has avoided the fate of many New Zealand small towns. The assiduously laid-out industrial estate, empty of industry for so many years, now boasts several small enterprises. The big catch, though, was the Advanced Foods works. This takes lamb and converts it into Bernard Matthews boneless roasts. Better, it means you can get a job in Waipuk. The factory now employs 250 people. A one-chain meatworks is in the wind. It would give work to 70 more. In a town of 4000 people, that is a lot of jobs. As for board-table dreams, the district's fortunes were always on the sheep's back.

This year's Weta festival began spectacularly, with Tim Wallis, the Luggate deer and helicopter magnate, crashing his newly acquired million dollar Spitfire at the town's airfield during a fund-raising event. Aerial adventures of this kind are not unknown in Waipukurau. Once, one of the topdressing pilots in town got into an argument with a garage owner. The pilot loaded his aeroplane's hopper and topdressed the garage with sheep manure. Everyone in town thought it was very funny, except for the pilot, who found himself in court, and the garage owner, who spent the weekend digging little knobs of dung out of his lube bay.

The arts festival ends with the debate in the cattle rostrum. It is one of those debates where no human orifice is left unexplored and the audience, who paid $20 a head, love it. In solid Nat country they are fascinated by Michael Laws, the party researcher who feeds Winston Peters his lines. Laws demonstrates that someone who pinches one joke is a plagiarist, but one who rustles a whole lot of them is a researcher. After a couple of speeches everyone goes out to relieve themselves. The men stand on the catwalks above the yards. Some of the women climb down into the yards themselves. They seem very brave. The Weta festival may not yet have made Waipukurau the cultural centre of New Zealand, but it is definitely on its way.

The strange ways of New Zealand small towns are not always properly celebrated. Waipukurau had a split personality. On one side the farmers, businesspeople, established citizenry. On the other the transients. The population was kept in balance by newcomers arriving at the same rate escapees were breaking out. Lawyers, car sales people, agricultural advisors, reporters, hotel managers, drivers, clerks, schoolteachers, nurses came, served their time and left. God knows why we came or where most of us went; I only met one of them again, a bank manager who had turned to running a motor camp in Nelson.

Shortly after midnight last month Sergeant Russ Chant was called out by someone who had heard glass breaking behind the sports shop. Bingo, there was a stolen car outside and a bloke—from out of town, Chant emphasised later—loading it with stolen sports bags. Before Chant could ask him to help with his inquiries the villain pointed an antique shotgun and forced the sergeant to let him escape. A fine old hunt followed and the man was eventually caught, far away.

To old Waipuk hands, life went on as usual. Shortly before I first arrived in town Sergeant Jack Bryant, then heading a local squad of two constables, had interrupted a burglary at a home appliance store. The thieves were busy manhandling a fridge out of the first-floor showroom and off the verandah roof when Bryant arrived.

The story goes that Bryant roared, 'Drop it!', so the crooks did. Bryant was lucky to escape unhurt.

I gathered two things from the incident. The first was that Waipukurau was not the one-level place it had first seemed to be. So it proved. Life was more often bizarre than mundane. It seemed to me that the town bred desperation in its citizens, a sense of living in a closed compartment, producing curious behaviour unknown in cities. The second was that we had a rather odd police sergeant.

The popular view is that country police officers cut parental figures in their communities. Perhaps some do. To me they were like floorwalkers in a department store; they made you feel guilty.

Bryant had few points of contact with the town. Many did not even go through the motions of being polite to him. His two constables were more user-friendly. One was a soft-looking man with a face like a mushroom and a genial, slow manner. Someone put a shot through his house window one night but the constable was so inoffensive it was generally reckoned to have been an accident. The other was an alert man who might even have been one of the boys had he not been a constable. He was beaten up once by a gang of youths

from Hastings whom he had ejected from a bar. When the bar patrons heard of this they were so indignant about *their* cop being beaten up that they went after the Hastings bunch and gave them a hiding.

Both constables treated Bryant as if he were an unexploded bomb. The sergeant frightened me. He could be friendly, or amiable, rather, but his eyes would not follow suit. They were for looking out of only. He appeared to live in a place a few centimetres behind them, so they had a mechanical appearance. He was not even indifferent. He just seemed to be somewhere else.

He was called to a burglary in the wine shop one night. He hurried along with his Browning semi-automatic pistol, which he later said in court he often took with him on such missions. He discovered a youth in the act of helping himself to the grog. The intruder took one look as Bryant leapt into action, and hurled a screwdriver. It struck the sergeant in the head, flooring him. The thief escaped, amid bullets.

Bryant told the court later that, weakened by the blow, he'd thought the suspect might wrest his pistol from him. No thief on his patch would go about armed at police expense, Bryant decided, and he'd emptied the gun into the surrounds.

Of course, it was hard to keep that quiet, when the police were supposed to be unarmed and shootouts were still rare; especially in a town whose visiting magistrate presided over a monthly court list of mainly pub fights and DICs. So police headquarters patted him on the back, a little reluctantly I thought, and everyone had their day in court.

The burglar described his fright at seeing the sergeant coming at him with a gun. He'd panicked, thrown the screwdriver and fled. But here was Bryant bearing the scar and the man in the dock was patently the culprit.

Being 50 km from home seemed to diminish Bryant.

Apparently knowing no one in court, not even other police officers, he seemed no more menacing than an authoritarian teacher unexpectedly met at the beach.

Bryant was waiting for me outside the court during one lunch break, holding open the door of his Mark 2 Zephyr so I had no choice but to get in. His eyes were watery.

He wanted to know what people in Waipukurau thought of him. I stammered a few meaningless words but he wasn't listening anyway. He needed to tell me the only thing he wanted from the town. 'Respect,' he said. 'That's what I want.'

Sergeant Russ Chant, though, found a different way of earning it.

Chant believes that city constables on the beat who have their minds in neutral may as well not be there. He tells his constables they must first look the part. Then they must walk down one side of the street as if they own it, looking at the other side as if they are going to buy it. They must talk to people in the street, get to know them, make them into eyes and ears.

He pays a lot of attention to the town's kids, especially those at risk. He reverses the tendency to pour resources into people who have already offended. Chant believes that young people who get into trouble are often rewarded, maybe a new jacket and a stay at a health camp to boast about. He makes role models for at-risk kids by rewarding those who do no wrong.

When Chant arrived in Waipukurau in late 1987, there were 42 major charges in a six-week period in November-December: six cases of fraud, seven burglaries, 11 assaults, drugs, a threat to kill, an armed kidnapping. Last year the district court judges found themselves spending 21 per cent less time in the Waipukurau courthouse. In the three years prior to 1988 the Waipukurau children's court averaged 89 cases. Last year the total was only 42.

Chant's methods have attracted a lot of attention nationally. As for Waipukurau, I spoke to one of Bryant's most ardent adversaries. Chant, he declared, was not a bad bloke. It was quite an accolade.

The back of the Wanstead Hotel looks like a desert but the proprietor is pleased with himself. He has just held what he hopes will be the first annual Wanstead axemen's festival. What is more, he had not chopped for 30 years but reckons he performed so well the opposition just rolled tits-up. 'I murdered them.'

On the other hand, things are not so good at this exact moment. He has just taken some hangi stones back to Porangahau and you gather he'd dallied. There has been a family argument. He is the head honcho but he has to look after the bar when he really wants a snooze. Meanwhile, why don't we look at these snaps of logs being hacked about?

After the debate that night there is a party where we are interrupted by a woman whose piercing voice cuts into the conversation like the publican's axe. Eventually she accuses us of not being farmers and stalks off. It is reassuring to find local customs so well preserved.

You can still drive out of Waipukurau past the old Pukeora home for the disabled, scene of a great local scandal when the hospital board eventually succeeded in evicting a disabled resident, but not before he'd locked himself in and broadcast his story on his ham radio.

When I left Waipukurau for good I drove through that gully, looking at hills burned yellow in the summer, and the bright, bright blue sky above them. It was pretty but I resolved never to go back. A long time later both sides are a lot less harsh in their judgements.

In the Wake
of the Whales

bruce ansley
photographer: bruce foster
6 may 1991

Just offshore, tourists wonder at the majesty of giant sperm whales. The whales have brought the town of Kaikoura millions of dollars—plus intrigue, envy, racism and sabotage.

You know a town is getting on when it gets its first wholefoods restaurant. Maybe high fibre gets a place moving. For years, Kaikoura's only claim on passing gourmets was its boiled crays. Now it has two licensed restaurants and a cafe selling spinach lasagne. It also has three new subdivisions. Property values are up by a quarter and two of the most-used words in town are 'no vacancy'. Kaikoura is boom amid gloom. It has streets full of Japanese, American and German accents, and a tidy trade in Queenstown-style rumours of coming developments—and talk of a vendetta in its rich new industry.

The town owes everything to a vagary of the Continental shelf, which edges to within a kilometre of the shore here. From the road which winds through tunnels and around the bluffs of this eternally sparkling coast you can see the deep pelagic blue where the ocean floor plunges 2000 m—as deep as the Kaikoura mountains on the other side of the road are high.

Here the cold current sweeping northwards along the Canterbury coast meets the warmer water from the north. They converge in a giant upwelling from the mountainous seafloor, spawning marine life which gives Kaikoura a unique attraction: it's the only place in the world where you can step into a small boat, go a little way offshore, and see a sperm whale.

So the world has begun beating a path to Kaikoura to see the majestic spectacle of a fluke rising against the snowy peaks. Tourists are almost always stirred by the sight; and, more crucial to the industry, they get out of the boats 75 bucks lighter and still smiling.

In the past three years a big industry has grown up around the whales: the four whale-watching boats gross more than $2m a year. A helicopter and two aeroplanes have permits to carry tourists to the whales; and three boats offer diving among the dolphins and seals. The town's take, for accommodation, food, petrol and services, is much more. A conservative multiplier doubles the gross from the whales, so the town's share is at least $4m, probably $5m or more.

Kaikoura should be content, but many in the town are not. The whale-watching industry has some very unusual elements. The largest company in the business started out as an employment project for jobless Maori and now has a monopoly. The industry is effectively controlled by the Department of Conservation (DoC), whose concern is to protect the whales, while a dozen supplicants cIamour to get in on the money.

At one level it's a model of care and conservation. On another, behind every happy tourist there's intrigue, envy, racism, sabotage. Plenty of people want in and it's a small town. Big fish, small pond.

Conflicting stories tell of how it all began. The charitable view is that a beam of light seemed to hit two groups simultaneously.

Barbara and Roger Sutherland had been thinking about the whales' tourist potential since 1985; but they wanted to take people out in commercial fishing boats and their problem was that the Ministry of Transport wouldn't let them because there is no safe harbour in Kaikoura.

Originally from San Francisco, Barbara is a naturalist who had been researching whales and came here to work on the sperm whales. She has the earnest manner of a 60s idealist and dislikes admissions of conflict. Here she met Roger, a fisherman, and worked on his boat. They married.

These two knew Kaikoura had something: besides whales, there are dolphins, penguins, seals, albatrosses, all neatly enclosed in one of the world's spectacular arenas.

About the same time, Bill Solomon was thinking he really should be doing something with these whales he'd known about all his life. Solomon had dreams but no money.

One day he was sitting at his Takahanga marae, site of the ancient Takahanga pa until its Ngai Tahu inhabitants were dislodged by Te Rauparaha's Ngati Toa. (Of course, the Ngai Tahu later evicted the Ngati Toa from the South Island.) Des Snelling came by.

Snelling was a banker, retired from Westpac, and he was at a loose end. 'Have a cup of tea, mate,' said Solomon. 'I hear you're interested in developing your marae,' said Snelling. Solomon: 'That's right. Full of dreams and no money.' Said Snelling: 'Let me handle the money. You handle the dreams.'

Kaikoura wasn't doing so well at the time. With the public service and the railways in full retreat and the fishing industry grappling with the quota system, jobs were thinner than Mrs Shipley's grin. But Solomon remembered how well the young people had done as guides for the *Te Maori* exhibition. 'I thought, if we could get into tourism . . .'

Taking people to see the whales seemed a good idea. With

Solomon: 'That's right. Full of dreams and no money.' Said Snelling: 'Let me handle the money. You handle the dreams.'

Solomon now employed through the Internal Affairs Department as an employment officer, the marae group raised equity capital through housie, bottle drives and, in some cases, mortgaging their homes.

Meanwhile the Sutherlands were working with the marae on a study. Could the marae group set up a business taking people to see the whales, and make money? But in the event it was the Sutherlands who first walked out of DoC's office with a permit to watch the whales for their own company, Nature Watch. 'It looked like their programme was a good year away, whereas we could start virtually immediately,' says Barbara Sutherland. Goaded into action, Solomon was hot on their heels, having raised enough, according to Snelling, 'to go to sea with one boat, a few brochures and a lot of hope. . .'

The business took off. 'We got busy,' says Sutherland. 'We didn't have time for anything. It wasn't just mom and pop going out in a casual sense. You're hiring staff. You're on the 'phone from six in the morning until 10 or 11 at night.'

The Sutherlands got a second boat added to their permit. So did Kaikoura Tours, Solomon's group, DoC sticking conscientiously to its ideal of a 50-50 treaty partnership.

The permits themselves are interesting documents. They're actually licences to 'harass the whales' under the Marine Mammals Protection Act. The whales fall into DoC's ambit. DoC didn't know much: 'about whale-watching at the time but knew what it didn't like: harassment of the whales in Alaska, where 21 companies compete for passengers, or in Hawaii, where vessels can carry 100 people at a time.

DoC determined to proceed warily. Two permits, for four small boats carrying a dozen passengers each, seemed a small enough operation while they waited to see what would happen. 'It wasn't obvious at that stage it was going to boom the way it has,' says Mike Donoghue, principal conservation officer for marine mammals. 'I thought, "If they get to take 50 tourists between them they'll be doing well . . ."'

What happened was that business took off. 'From the beginning we saw it was a pandora's box,' says Sutherland. 'We had no personal life. We couldn't go anywhere.' The Sutherlands had imagined a cruisy life taking out, perhaps, a couple of boatloads a day, five days a week but they were soon working an 18-hour day, seven days a week, when they really wanted to sail their yacht to Tonga.

By this time, those permits to harass were being seen more as licences to print money. When the Sutherlands decided they had other things they wanted to do with their lives, two big bidders knocked on their door; one, Barbara Sutherland claims, overseas-owned and well-heeled.

But the Sutherlands wanted the business to stay with local people who would look after their whales. 'We didn't want this to turn into a THC [Tourist Hotel Corporation], or go to an overseas concern which wants to put up a big hotel.'

They turned down the dollars being fluttered at them and sold instead to the local party, Kaikoura Tours, for what Sutherland claims was a much lower figure. To raise the money Kaikoura Tours called in the Ngai Tahu Trust Board as a partner.

Bill Solomon became boss of what may well be New Zealand's most successful employment project. And Kaikoura Tours, the company that started on the marae, had a monopoly on the country's fastest-growing business.

Even in Wellington there's a hint of embarrassment about this. After all, those permits say at the bottom, 'Not transferrable'. Kaikoura Tours took over Nature Watch and the permit remains in Nature Watch's name; it's all legal, and DoC chose the view that whatever private arrangement the two companies came to may be the Ministry of Commerce's business but it wasn't DoC's.

In Kaikoura the reaction was less delicate. Sutherland says no one else besides Kaikoura Tours was rushing forward with their cheque books open when they decided to sell. 'We were pretty open in saying we were interested in moving on. It wasn't like there was any secret squirrel stuff.' But Kaikoura is a small town.

There are now 12 applicants for new permits. Some have been waiting for more than a year. Simple arithmetic sorts out the figures: 25–30,000 passengers a year at $75 a head comes to $2m plus annually.

It's true that outgoings are high. The boats cost almost $100,000 each with spares and land transport. They wear out quickly, bouncing around the open sea at high speeds, and use a lot of fuel. Kaikoura Tours is what economists call labour-intensive, but Bill Solomon calls simple job creation: with allied businesses they employ some 46 people. Solomon himself, now a manager in the upwardly mobile bracket, draws no salary from the company; he's still a paid employment officer. He sits in his small office in the old Kaikoura railway station (which is now painted bright blue), with his feet up on the most dominant piece of furniture after the two computers, a large plastic rubbish bin.

But there's still a tidy profit in the whales and someone in town cracked nasty. First, they pulled out all the gearbox plugs in all eight outboard motors. When the boats put to sea, salt water mixed with the oil and ruined the gearbox units. Then they burnt the company's 44-seater bus. After that, Kaikoura Tours' insurance company refused to insure them.

Someone in town doesn't like Kaikoura Tours' success and the odd thing, in such a small town, is that the police have no leads on who it is. 'With a serious incident like this,' says Constable Murray Devine, 'people are frightened to approach the police.'

Bill Solomon's best bet is that it is a nutter—'but a dangerous nutter. Maybe even one of those greenie nutters who write to us saying we're damaging the whales.' But one with the technical expertise to work out such an efficient means of sabotage as removing the gearbox bungs?

A jealous competitor then, with a racist edge? Racist? Solomon takes a while to answer. 'It's the first thing that runs through your mind. I'd hate to think it was.' But this town is no different from a lot of others, with its share of bigotry, and you don't have to be long in a pub to hear something racist about Kaikoura Tours.

'If you really want my opinion,' says Barbara Sutherland, who has spent a little time telling me why the media shouldn't go stirring things up, 'I was *staggered* at the racism when Kaikoura Tours started their operation. I was staggered at the things that were said to us in the street, or in the pub. We just stopped socialising. We got sickened, quite frankly. I mean, *we* were the ones who should have been against Kaikoura Tours. How much shit do you think would be happening right now if Roger and I had the monopoly? Not nearly as much, believe me.'

Des Snelling, the ex-banker who popped in to help because he liked their spirit, believes he has seen the ugly side of small-town New Zealand. 'There has been an orchestrated campaign by a small number of people to discredit Kaikoura Tours with the purpose of getting a licence themselves.'

The constituents of Kaikoura Tours just can't win. Once derided for being on the dole, now they're scorned for their success.

Evidence that the watchers may be upsetting the whales has brought the industry to a crisis-point. A report shows that speeding skippers are causing the whales to take evasive action.

Researchers Jane MacGibbon from Canterbury University and Scott Baker, a world authority on humpback whales who is at present on a fellowship at Victoria University, identified three groups of whales: the shy whales of winter, the more plentiful, more approachable whales of summer, and the resident animals such as the famous 'Hoon', which will seek out boats.

The report found that the winter and summer sperm whales were avoiding the high-speed outboard-powered boats of the watchers by shallow diving. The whales' surface movements became erratic; their respiratory rate rose. These effects, the researchers found, were compounded by bad driving; speeding up to the whales, speeding too close to them, accelerating only seconds after the whales dived.

Kaikoura is a stopping-off point on a migration route and the whales are not endangered by the watchers, just worried; but DoC is taking the view that it should minimise the difficulty. The curious thing about the MacGibbon report is that, having fretted over the effect on the whales, the MacGibbon report then envisages a further one, perhaps two, permits being issued.

The apparent contradiction arises because DoC is

'What we've got . . . is a lot of young boys yupping around in boats at full tilt without paying a lot of attention to doing a good interpretative service.'

worried about inexperienced young skippers. A number of people, including some environmentally minded tourists, have kept a critical eye on the whale-watchers. 'What we've got,' said one observer, 'is a lot of young boys yupping around in boats at full tilt without paying a lot of attention to doing a good interpretative service.' Gordon O'Callahan, a Kaikoura Tours driver until he was sacked a few weeks ago when Solomon discovered he was one of the applicants for a permit, says he was taught by the Sutherlands to be careful, to be an expert on what he was showing the tourists. 'That's not the philosophy of the young skippers. They chase everything that blows. They think the only way to travel is flat out. They have no time to talk to people.'

Barbara Sutherland agrees that everyone gets it wrong sometimes: 'None of us are wearing totally white hats out there on the water.' Warnings have been issued to at least one driver, although Andrew Baxter, DoC's senior conservation' officer, coastal marine in Nelson, will say only that, 'We're in communication to ensure that the regulations are followed strictly.' The ultimate sanction is to revoke the permit. Clearly, DoC doesn't want to do that; it believes that Kaikoura Tours'

operation is good, if only it would pull its skippers into line.

But Solomon is angry, over both the report and DoC's warnings. His drivers (who, says O'Callahan, can average $1200–$1400 a week in summer) would never do anything to affect the whales: 'You build up such a relationship.'

Solomon, meanwhile, is hoping to 'drive a truck' through the MacGibbon report. He questions its methods. He alleges a vendetta against his company and its drivers. He is threatening to sue for compensation if more licences are issued, to seek an injunction against DoC, to pursue a claim under the Treaty: 'Who the hell are you to tell us what to do with this resource? When you prove to us you own it, then you can talk about it.' Solomon hopes it won't come to that. 'It's not very nice,' he says, and then, so softly I hardly hear him, adds, 'Hell, they'll probably burn us out.'

And why not a monopoly? he asks. Look at the Milford Track, the Hollyford. Now they're successful. I wonder, why should we expect his company to behave differently from any other successful company whose business is threatened?

Solomon doesn't seem to be enjoying himself. He feels under attack from all sides and 37 families depend on him for jobs. 'All we did,' he says, 'was create a business'.

Boar Wars

steve braunias
photographer: jenny scown
17 july 1993

Everyone knows it is possible to eat, sweat, stink, snore and bleed like a pig. But I was unprepared when Brian Crow, twice former champion of the annual Tikorangi wild boar hunt, told me during his attempt to win the 1993 title: 'You have to think like a pig.'

I suppose I should have responded with a grunt, which might suggest an ability to get a fix on the dark, remote world of a pig's mind. However, until I crashed about the Taranaki bush with Crow's team over Queen's Birthday weekend, the closest I'd been to a wild boar was the great stuffed head mounted above the television at his Uruti farmhouse. This monster had won him the 1990 trophy. Its open-mouthed tusks and beady little eyes greet all who come through the front door; once composed, visitors can watch other boars caught and slaughtered on a bunch of terrifically vivid home videos. A shaky picture witnesses the frenzied kill, but the sound quality is clear: the dying pig's squeal so curdling and close that Crow's dog, Joy, will run in from the porch and is stirred barking mad.

Mere home comforts. Sixty teams of three hunters set outdoors for the wettest competition since it started in 1982 as a fundraiser for the Tikorangi rugby club. Organisers clocked up 750 km in a poster-run of North Island pubs, bringing in entries from Whangarei to Wairoa. The rules are plain enough ('All pigs must be fully gutted with the head and tail left on . . . participants enter at their own risk'), but a controversial chain of events has led to this year's major prize of $500 and three Swanndris going to the team whose pig is closest to the average weight of all captured beasts.

Some hunters grumbled that it reduced the contest to a lottery. Letters were sent out to explain: 'Prizes for the heaviest boars have been downgraded to try and discourage people from trying to rip off the honest hunter by weighing in illegal pigs.'

Only a few years ago it was discovered that the heaviest boar had actually been bought from the Otorohonga saleyards and calmly killed to win the trophy. And last year Crow and his team were nearly pipped at the post by a porkier pig, until growing suspicion of its smooth snout and trotters indicating it was bred in domestic bliss, led a to disqualification.

Crow's team-mate, Waitara freezing-worker Alan 'Bisto' Bisson, was especially relieved to win. Their boar outweighed the impostor at the kill, but then lost a vital kilo of blood because, Crow fumed, Bisto had hung it up 'the wrong bloody way' overnight. Although the trophy cooled his fury, Crow is still testy when the matter of wasted splatter is raised.

Crow, Bisto and third hunter Okau farmer Guy Selby were prepared for the 1993 event. Separately they killed about four decent-sized boars leading up to the hunt, and made checks on likely gullies. They had the bait: wild goats, which used to fetch up to $250 but are worthless these days, were shot, gutted and laid out in the bush. They had the knives, the dogs, the experience. They also had a heavy-smoking slob from the city, dressed up in the same clothes he'd worn to a respectable bar the previous night, as a passenger. They seemed worried. At least I wasn't a vegetarian.

Uruti is a small but lively farming community set in a picturesque valley, where moonlight glitters on the shuffling mists, and the quacking of wild ducks can be the only sound for many still hours. It also rains a lot. Just as we set off from Crow's house at 8.00 am it begins to hose down, and never lets up. Think like a pig? After we park in steep back-country, cross a swollen stream, examine untouched dead sheep and goats, scale fences, avoid stinging nettles, use planks to surf over swamps, and crash our way to the top of a ridge as the rain pours buckets, about all I can think of is a warm bed.

'Thinking of a warm bed?' Bisto laughs.

Paddocks spread out beneath the ridge, and dip towards a gully to the east. A flock of sheep makes a sudden bolt, but it's more significant that a herd of goats is obviously avoiding even the fringes of the gully. Further down, it seems as if a pig has rooted about in some cowpats, looking for worms. In low, murmured voices we are discussing the freshness of other markings, when the dogs begin to bark. The cry goes up: 'Pig!' With ridiculous speed, the team crash into the bush just as a high, terrified, impossible squeal shrieks out. Selby and two dogs are on top of a pig. Crow and Bisto bash on towards another commotion. Selby wrestles with the pig as it drags him down the bank. The dogs lock a savage grip on its ears, its snout. A knife slashes into and across the pig's throat. The damp ground is painted red. As calmly as if he wants me to help wash the dishes, Selby asks, 'Can you lend us a hand?' while the squeals continue to penetrate the centre of the earth. Looping a roll of twine around the neck of the most ferocious dog, who has bitten so deep that it has mangled the pig's bones, I strangle and pull until it finally releases its hold.

The pig is dead. It's a fat sow, not qualified for the hunt, which Selby has killed to put his dogs onto the other chase. Down below, where Crow has fallen into a stream, he and Bisto are trying to call off their dogs: it's another sow. I go back to see Selby slit open the belly-up sow and reach in to spill out its guts. He fossicks about to grab onto a few other bits and bloody pieces. The intestines wriggle on the ground, and settle to a bloody pulp.

'Reach in if you want,' he says. 'It'll warm up your hands.' In the quiet, sweet-smelling bush, Selby ties up the sow and piggy-backs it up to the paddock. As he climbs, the sow's head bounces merrily on his shoulder, and rain washes hot blood down the back of his coat.

We meet Crow on the other side of the gully, and shelter under a dead, blackened tree. A lone hawk soars above the stark landscape—Vincent Ward filmed *Vigil* in Uruti—while we wait for Bisto to emerge. 'Two heads are about to pop up,' Crow predicts. In fact, only one arrives. Bisto has kept his, and hacked off the sow's. Crow asks what took him so long. Bisto replies that it was a steep climb, and at one point he was hanging on with his life at the end of a vine. A man dangling in the air with a headless sow tied to his back: pig-hunting has its comic moments.

No boar wars that day. The dogs raced after and killed a baby pig, while Crow rescued another which had deep wounds to its left shoulder, and a third from the litter followed us with pathetic trust. I cradled these squirming, shivering survivors along a ridge, while the team found an enormous 70 kg sow charging at their nervous dogs.

'Watch yourself,' Selby warned. This was good advice, as the furious sow may have been the mother of my armload. A wild sow can cause enough damage—even a domestic pig recently managed to gore and kill a 60-year-old Canterbury man—and boars are hardly shy to attack a man on his own. Selby had come out looking for a lost dog the previous week when he turned to see a boar thundering at his heels. There was no time to head for the hills. No time for anything, in fact, but to swing a leg and kick it in the head. The boar buzzed off. Selby likes a game of league now and then.

We returned at 3.00 p.m. I scoffed a plate of spaghetti, wondering why the wriggling mound seemed so recently familiar, and preferred to doze as the team rode their farm bikes to another gully. That night, their headlights flashed up in the dense valley, where they had killed only a small boar.

As for the three little pigs, I had put the untouched baby back in the bush, Selby stuffed the corpse into his dead sow's

'Two heads are about to pop up,' Crow predicts. In fact, only one arrives. Bisto has kept his, and hacked off the sow's.

gutted belly, and Crow gave the fawn-coloured survivor a shot of penicillin at his farm, before placing it with wool in a barrel. By morning it had died.

Meanwhile, I had gorged myself on wild pork, and sprang out of bed at 5.00 a.m., ready for blood.

We headed towards the coast. Nothing happened. A marking here and there; difficult to say how fresh because of the rain, which also threw off the scent. A dead sheep had been dragged down a ridge and ripped open, probably the day before; but nothing stirred.

Beside a stream, among tangled supplejack, there was plenty of stirred mud; but no evidence that a pig had rubbed its coated hide up against any ponga trees.

Pig intellect and tracking skills aside, a successful hunt depends on good dogs, and plain good luck. Right time, right place, a sudden scent. It could be we were jinxed from the start. Travelling down by bus, my ill-equipped nose led me to the Te Kuiti tea-rooms, where an unlikely party of five chortling men in grey suits and grey winter faces spread themselves over two tables. Chief of the chortling chums was the Prime Minister. He sipped his tea, gargled on his consonants and, as he left, fixed me with a sour look. In the 220nd anniversary year of Captain Cook introducing a boar and several sows to New Zealand, I knew the hunt was doomed.

Mmmmm, smell that bacon. On the 4.00 p.m. judging deadline there are 23 boars stacked in a row across a plank on the back of a truck at the Tikorangi clubrooms.

More than 1000 people have turned up, and passed in front of the pageant of death, noting the wounds, the tusks—frowns of examination inches away from the boars' pleasant grinning faces.

Appropriately, the winner of the man-against-beast event is on crutches. Taumarunui mechanic Shane Rix, who took the 1991 trophy, baled the 86.8 kg boar in Ongarue. It broke away four times, gored three dogs, and finally squealed its last a kilometre away down in the creek. As for Rix, he owed his wounds to a manuka stake, which cut open his shin as he carried his beast through a swamp.

Two old-time pig-hunters, and a meat inspector, are on hand to make sure there has been no foul play. 'We try to run a tight bloody honest competition,' say organisers Fred Quilter and Ross Potier, 'and it looks like this year went off pretty bloody well. A bugger about the rain, but it's turned out to be a bloody good day.' Good for the hunters, good for the club. Over the years, their fundraising efforts have helped to build excellent clubrooms, with a gym, a bar, and a considerate set of membership rules: 'Please moderate your language as ladies are always present.'

The prizes, totalling $1800 in cash, are given with rich Kiwi praise ('Way to go, fella! . . . Well, hurry up here'), and the crowd drift into a tent for beer and a delicious hangi of potatoes, chicken, pumpkin, kumara and wild pork. It looks like a long night, and perhaps not without incident; at last year's awards, a local petrol station was robbed.

I look back to the valley when my bus leaves the following morning. Of course, pig-hunting is cruel, vicious, bloodthirsty. But it's a compulsive sport. I head home, and keep looking at the hills, the bush, watching for movement, wanting to return.

Arson at Okarito

bruce ansley
photographer: bruce foster
9 september 1995

Once endangered by logging, the rare white heron now faces fire and feud.

The first white herons have appeared at Okarito. The pure-white kotuku are wearing their courting dress, long dorsal plumes filigreed behind their tails. For the next six months they will mate, nest and breed near the mouth of the Waitangiroto River, at the north end of the Okarito lagoon in South Westland. Up to 50 pairs of birds will nest here, in the only kotuku breeding colony in New Zealand—a precarious sanctuary, less than two kilometres from the Tasman Sea, and vulnerable to the wild westerly storms that roar off the sea in spring.

But this year they face new threats: twin, man-made perils of fire and feud.

Locals are torching tracts of reserve land in protests aimed at the Department of Conservation (DoC). A blaze in August swept through 150 ha of pakihi swamp bordering the white herons' reserve. Firefighters say it needed only a wind change to fan the flames five kilometres through the forest to the birds' refuge.

Meanwhile, the sanctuary tour operator, Ken Arnold, is involved in a local dispute of his own. He has been assaulted twice, his wife has been spat at, his car damaged. His whitebaiter's bach has been razed.

In Whataroa, the town nearest the breeding colony, the atmosphere is obdurate. The town is a gaggle of houses, a school, a couple of shops and a garage spread along the highway. Locals pronounce the name as it was misspelt until 1934, Wataroa. Newcomers who call the town *Phut*aroa are instantly suspect; although, like most West Coast small towns, this one treats strangers with reserve anyway.

The tiny town sits among some of the world's finest scenery—lakes, beaches, the road tunnelling through virgin forest in places. Some townspeople are paranoid. About DoC, which it sees as ruled by fumbling Wellington bureaucrats; about the growing power of the green movement, which it suspects wants to lock it in an economic straitjacket; about the feud between the Arnolds and another old Whataroa family, the McBrides, which it worries will escalate.

Whataroa is at a low point in its history. Some see it as the town's nadir.

Timber, the industry that bankrolled the town for much of its life, has slowly run out like the gold before it. Paynter's sawmill, which once employed 43 people, laid off 10 in July and there are now only 18 left. The native timber has run out. The mill has to rely on exotics. Another black mark for conservation.

Eco-tourism, or nature tourism, is the new growth industry in the region. But some Coasters, the old guard, see only what they've lost. They blame the conservation lobby for the loss of their staple industry and refuse to recognise, yet, what they might gain.

Anti-green sentiment is always strong on the West Coast. The most commonly heard statistic in Whataroa is that only seven per cent of South Westland is privately owned—DoC owns the rest.

Coasters have seen DoC as joining with conservation groups to shut away their natural resources—the forests, rivers, minerals, even the fresh water that they hope to export to thirsty Gulf states.

They've reacted in the traditional way. Fires are second nature to them; they've always burned the swamp country to encourage new growth and now, to protest, they simply grab a box of matches.

Says Brian McBride: 'People down here have the stitch with DoC—you have to understand that. They affect a lot of people's livelihood. So people are using fires as a way of getting back at DoC. They're ticked with DoC and they know every time they light one, DoC has to spend $20,000 putting it out.'

In fact, DoC spends at least that. The 12 months to June cost the department a record $1.3m for fighting 211 fires on the land it controls throughout the country. Twenty-three of those fires, more than any other area except Nelson-Marlborough, were lit on the West Coast.

The Okarito-Whataroa area has had more than its share of fires, 11 since 1991 and four in the last year alone.

The last, in the pakihi swamp, with its fernbird and Australasian bittern habitats bordering the white heron sanctuary, was by far the most serious, although an earlier blaze in nine hectares of manuka scrub at the other end of the Okarito lagoon threatened a kiwi habitat.

Says DoC spokesman Steve Attwood: 'Fires are a cost, an inconvenience and a risk to life at times, but one of our biggest concerns is that people are damaging our national heritage. Precious wildlife habitat is being destroyed. They're not just hurting DoC, but national resources that, in some instances, are under threat. This last fire in the pakihi swamp was right on the border of the white heron reserve. People say West Coast bush doesn't burn; but it does and, in the right conditions, it can travel five kilometres very quickly. If the wind had been from a different quarter it could have blown the fire towards the white heron colony and, at one stage, our firefighters were considering that possibility.'

Attwood refuses to speculate on how many of the fires are anti-DoC—'it encourages others to do the same'—but, for locals, the issues are simple enough.

Jim Purcell is an old Coaster who once leased the pakihi swamp that was burnt in the latest fire. He torched it regularly himself to encourage growth and ease stock-handling. 'Burning was how New Zealand was started,' he says. 'It gave you extra grazing and only cost a box of matches.'

So Coasters didn't have to look far for a way of protesting against a government agency that they find over restrictive: 'The fires are because DoC hasn't got credibility, and once you lose that you're on a slippery slope,' says Purcell. 'They do the same thing in Ireland. Now, I'm not supporting any IRA kind of thing, but what other kind of protest can people do?'

Okarito, once a goldrush town and now a quiet seaside settlement housing 31 people, is only just down the road from Whataroa, but a long way from it in sentiment. Okarito, says Debbie McLachlan. who runs Okarito Nature Tours, is a green community. She has helped fight several of the fires in the last two years, fires that she believes are lit as an anti-green statement.

McLachlan has been threatened occasionally—once a fist was shaken in her face—but says things are changing, even down the road in conservative Whataroa. Trouble is, she says, some diehards haven't changed, hence the fires. Maybe, she hopes, they'll taper off: 'We're at the peak of the worst consequences arising from the change from a plundering policy to a sustainable management policy.'

Ian Price, the senior constable who represents the law in Whataroa, is certain that the latest fire, like many others, was deliberately lit, although he doesn't believe the fire-raisers intended either to strike back at DoC or endanger the white heron colony. That, however, *is* speculative. In his 12 years in

'People down here have the stitch with DoC—you have to understand that. So people are using fires as a way of getting back at DoC . . . they know every time they light one, DoC has to spend $20,000 putting it out.'

the town, Price has never been able to catch anyone illegally lighting fires.

The running feud is a side-issue. Ken Arnold owns White Heron Sanctuary Tours; Brian McBride is a helicopter operator. The two sides have conflicting stories on how the squabble began, but it escalated quickly. McBride and another man appeared in court after Arnold and his wife were assaulted. Arnold, a big man whose size is accentuated by his short hair and clipped moustache, refuses to speak about the affair. 'It's in the hands of the authorities.'

McBride insists the feud has nothing to do with the fires. For Arnold also had his whitebaiter's bach on the river burnt to the ground. He and a friend had had the place for 25 years —built illegally, says Arnold, 'like any other whitebaiter's bach on any of the rivers that are built on DoC land up and down the West Coast; there wouldn't be 10 of them that are legal'.

The bach was a big loss, says Arnold. Someone might have wanted to take a shot at him. Why? Says Arnold, cagily: 'Who knows?' But he argues that the fire had nothing to do with his business—or the white heron colony, and for once the antagonists agree. 'I've got nothing against white herons—the herons are not in any danger as far as I'm concerned,' says McBride.

The fire in the pakihi swamp was right next door to Arnold's operation, but Price insists that the two weren't connected. Arnold has a building and a jetty a short distance from where the fire was lit; yet Arnold's property was untouched. The tour operator, though, is worried: 'Let's face it, fires in nature reserve areas should be a worry to *everybody*.'

Others in the town are also nervous, for, as the timber runs out, Whataroa's fortunes are increasingly based on eco-tourism. 'It just needs a few more people to do what we're doing,' says McLachlan, 'for local people to see that it's no use plundering the resource.'

Arnold pays DoC for the right to take tourists into the kotuku colony and, by his own account, is doing very well out of it. When he started six years ago he took 800 people to see the birds; last year the number was 3500. This season he expects to hire five full-time and four part-time staff and hopes eventually to employ 10 full time. He now runs the biggest business in Whataroa except for the sawmill and, the way eco-tourism is shaping up against the timber industry, he could one day be tops. Local people have yet to appreciate the irony.

The Save Okarito campaign, when the forest and its sanctuary were threatened by logging, was one of this country's early environmental pitched battles. The conservationists won that one, but outbreaks of guerrilla warfare continue. Astonishingly, the kotuku remains unscathed—so far.

Heke's Hometown

keith stewart

photographer: debbie beadle

15 august 1998

Some call it the place where New Zealand started but Kaikohe now struggles to live up to its past.

James Belich's *New Zealand Wars* series offered me no historical surprises, but I have been troubled by the response from my fellow New Zealanders. I grew up in the Bay of Islands town of Kaikohe, once Hone Heke Pokai's home base, and I had always known that Heke and Kawiti completely outsmarted the British army, so I was rather bemused by claims that Belich was somehow distorting the truth to accord with some politically correct standard. The revelation was not Maori sagacity, but the habitual racism of Belich's critics, who strangely assume that the British army was 'us', and Heke 'them'.

Now that Belich has positioned Maori firmly at the centre of our history, and done so in the bathroom glare of television, perhaps we are at last ready to celebrate our own story, and recognise exactly who it is we are. If so, one place where such recognition might begin is my old hometown, where figures such as Kohuru te Whata, Hongi Hika, Hone Heke Pokai, Hone Heke, Hone Tuwhare and Johnny Smith have conferred a national resonance far greater than the town's size would suggest.

So I headed back north, looking for signs that the country could at last be coming to its cultural senses and that the real Kaikohe had some hope of discarding its contemporary media image as a drug-infused rural slum. I could see no reason why it should not become instead a place of significance; it was, after all the centre of the world when I was seven. Even in retrospect, it has a lot going for it—it is beautifully located and surprisingly rich in resources, even without its history.

Driving back in the green of winter, it was reassuring to see that the beauty hadn't faded, although the town had shrunk somewhat, as revisited hometowns do, and there is a quiet drabness about it that I don't remember. There was always promise here, and a sense of purpose, but that seems to have ebbed away with the town's industry, which was already dying with the kauri forests when I was a kid scrounging timber offcuts to give shape to my imagination. When the last block of bush was felled, so, too, were Kaikohe's sawmills, and now people wait for the pine forests to return some sawdust prosperity. But the railway has gone, and nobody can decide what will happen to the logs due in 2005. Shipped direct to Japan, or trucked further south, perhaps.

The decision is unlikely to be taken locally, which is the real problem, according to Laurie Byers, a one-time road cycling star, who now farms just beyond the town boundary on the property where he was raised. As one of Kaikohe's representatives on the Far North District Council, he laments the bleeding that his town has done in the wake of closure: dairy factory, airport, railway, bus services, telephone exchange.

'We should be a rich place. There is timber at our doorstep, the soil and the climate grow things faster than anywhere else in the country, we have plenty of labour. There is no reason for Kaikohe to be suffering like it does, but we need investment, we need outsiders to come in and help us tap into all the wealth we have. The problem is, we are the forgotten part of New Zealand, except in the holidays, when everybody comes up and pummels our roads and services for a few weeks.

'Sadly, some of our problem is a racial thing; they see us as a Maori place,' admits Byers. 'We have lost a lot of people from Kaikohe to Kerikeri from white flight, which is regrettable, because the Maori culture is a good culture and this is an important cultural town. This is where Hongi Hika taught his warriors to shoot his new muskets, it was his base through all those wars. Kaikohe was the centre of the Ngapuhi world, and the hub of New Zealand history in the first 50 years of European history. If you think about it, this is where New Zealand started.

It seems that some people don't want to think about it. The history of Kaikohe is unknown to most of its Pakeha citizens, who would be surprised to discover that there was a meeting in the town between leading Ngapuhi rangatira, including Tamati Waka Nene, Patuone and Hone Heke, in January 1840. Apparently, they discussed the impending arrival of Captain Hobson in the Bay of Islands, and their critical support for the Treaty of Waitangi probably had its foundations at that meeting.

It would be fair to assume that such an important location could be an attraction in Northland, where tourism rates as the second-largest industry, yet Kaikohe doesn't feature. Not much is made of the region's history yet, and most operators are keen to sell sea and sand and big-game fishing, rather than national pride.

The principal tourist sites in the North—Kerikeri, Paihia, Waitangi, Waimate North and Russell—are enclaves of Pakeha history in a profoundly Maori historical landscape, the neglect of which is as obvious and as tragic as the evacuation of industry from the district.

But, although tourism continues to ignore the richness of this other culture, there are signs that Ngapuhi are beginning to see possibilities here. At Kohiwhata, on the southern edge of the town, a bold new marae is being built that intends to realise some of that potential, not just in the elaborate carvings and architectural substance of classic Maori art, but in the activities planned around the marae.

'Here we are trying to create something, a precedent, not just from a business perspective, but for Maori, for marae around Kaikohe, around the North, and around the country. We have a lot of problems at various levels—our taonga, our wairua, our wananga, our reo, they have been suppressed for so long in the present system. But we have a system of our own, a Maori system, and our job is to put emphasis back into that, and to become effective and efficient in competing with mainstream businesses. The foundation of that must be Maori, and it must reverse the mainstream trend, which is to take Maori people away from the small, countrywide settlements and take them to the cities,' says the project co-ordinator, Miller Wihongi.

Ngapuhi kaumatua Graham Rankin acknowledges the efforts at Kohiwhata, but he believes that the problems Kaikohe faces are socio-economic, not racial, although they will become racial if local schools continue to lose community

The new marae.

The closed dairy factory.

support. Both the intermediate school and the secondary school are struggling to attract students, even with the town's population growing, and there is serious concern about educational standards at all levels.

To me, this is the biggest surprise in town, because my school memories are of a place that epitomised the imagined New Zealand where education was highly valued and schools were administered with a rough egalitarianism. Good schools defined Kaikohe, and Northland College, with its boarding facilities and 350 hectare farm, attracted students from around the Pacific Islands, as well as the North. But now the hostel is closed and the college roll has slumped to half its peak.

More than anything else, this slump in education symbolises Kaikohe's cultural dilemma, one that mirrors that of the whole country: the problem of uncertain identity and ignorance of the knowledge that defines us—history, art, ideas. Yet the schools seem unwilling to discuss the problem. The principal of Northland College, Jim Peters, turned me down when I rang him for an interview at an appointed time. Perhaps he was preoccupied with the independent review of the school currently in preparation.

Rankin is less circumspect on the issue: 'Education in this town is crazy. My granddaughter goes to the local kindergarten and it's all Maori children, because Pakehas are shifting their children somewhere else, because there's too many Maoris. This education thing is a big problem, and if we don't fix it we're in real trouble.'

'The school principals have to take some of the blame, but mostly it's the usual problem with low decile levels,' says teacher Te Tuhi Robust, highlighting the low socio-economic rankings (decile levels) of Kaikohe schools, which are below what the town's demographic profile would suggest. With access to wealthier school communities in nearby Kerikeri and Okaihau, parents simply bypass the issue of sending their children to a poor school.

'People move away to higher-rated schools, deciles drop further, and more people move away: it's a vicious cycle and, unless we get some improvement in the local economy, it's not going to change. We've got third-generation kids here whose parents have never known anything but the benefit, and dope is now a big problem that people won't face up to. At primary school, I know of 18 families whose kids have regular experience of dope at home; it's an accepted code of conduct. It's hard to get cultural pride when you're faced with that sort of social problem.'

Such problems have sharply focused the racial attitudes that have long been present in the town, making what was once a simple class division between labour and local business, easily defined by colour, into a tougher boundary enforced by the slur 'beneficiary'. Yet Kaikohe is still a two-tone town, Maori and Pakeha, with neither dominant.

'It is Maori that keep this town alive, even if it's benefit money they're spending,' says Rankin. The town's retailers have always known that, as memories of reaching into the greasy mutton bird barrel at Kennett's Grocery remind me. They are mostly Pakeha businesses, serving mostly Maori customers, and prosperous because of it.

'In Kaikohe there is still goodwill between Pakeha and Maori, and there is concern on both sides about crime and unemployed youth and drugs. It is fair to say that there are more extremes of attitude than there used to be, but under present social conditions that is to be expected,' says local stationer and bookseller Ray Clarke, who has lived most of his life in the town. He considers much of Kaikohe's image problem to be a media beat-up, rather than the reality of the place—one of the best business towns in the country.

'It may not be quite as good a place as it was, but in general Kaikohe does better than most other places. In fact, some say that Kaikohe is a better place to do business than Kerikeri, that there are more businesses teetering on the edge of viability in Kerikeri than there are here,' he says.

He also sees another reason to be confident about the town's future, and not just in business, but in the growing local awareness of the cultural importance of the district. 'There is much more awareness of Maori history and culture than there was when we were kids,' he says. 'The book titles in the shop reflect our strong Maori customer base, but it would also be fair to say that there is as much interest from Pakeha as there is from Maori. Our Maori section would compete with any other, including gardening and recipes. We even sell $60 or $70 books in reasonable quantities. *Redemption Songs*, for example; we sold six or seven of those, yet there are a lot of Paper Plus shops around the country that wouldn't even carry it in stock.'

Selling more books can't be a bad thing, but does it mean that the town, the country, is waking up to itself? That is not

The town's retailers have always known that, as memories of reaching into the greasy mutton bird barrel at Kennett's Grocery remind me.

the feeling you get from the shabby-looking buildings of the great Kotahitanga marae and the faded old Aperahama church nearby, nor as you pass the empty shops at the bottom of town. In the US or France, Kaikohe would be a place of pilgrimage, where we would take our families as an affirmation of citizenship. At the moment, travellers hardly stop long enough for a pie, leaving a feeling that something wonderful is being demeaned.

Before I go, I drive to the top of Kaikohe Hill for a final reflection. The carpark is much the same, but now the hill and its monument to the late 19th-century Kotahitanga MP Hone Heke has been refreshed with gardens and sweet paths, and there is a stone compass pointing out places of significant historical interest: the first Maori church, New Zealand's first dairy farm, Hongi's Pakinga Pa. Here, as a child, Hone Heke Pokai lived on bitter kohekohe berries while he and his hapu were under siege from Rewha Rewha of Ngati Whatua—kai kohekohe. I remember it as a place for a furtive booze binge and the chance of a back-seat fumble, but now it is asserting its mana. Maybe the bookseller is right, maybe things have changed. Perhaps next time that change will be more obvious.

Porirua,
Mon Amour

pamela stirling
photographer: bruce foster
19 september 1998

Cannon's Creek is drowsing in afternoon sunshine the day I drive cautiously into what *North & South* recently called this 'notorious', 'slum-like' suburb. This, the magazine reports, is a place where you 'lock the doors' in your car and put the windows up: 'It's frightening.' On last night's TV news I caught a glimpse of the old state house unit in which I lived for a couple of years as a child, and this morning I've heard on National Radio that now not even the poor want to live in these middle units of a block of four units. It sounds suspiciously like deprivation chic even to admit to it but I have this vague idea, I don't know . . . of knocking on the door of my old unit and asking the tenants if maybe they'd like me to buy some trees for what *North & South* dismisses as this 'barren' patch.

The tenants are not home, and I feel something like relief. I check out the Cannon's Creek Opportunity Centre instead. And, while I am there, among the women potting up gardening table cuttings, the toddlers playing with old toys and the young people hanging out on the worn couches or playing table tennis (there is 22 per cent unemployment here), some of the older Polynesian men who do the twice-daily voluntary Townwatch foot patrol come in for their cup of tea and cards. Today, it turns out, there is no money for milk for their tea. I produce the small change for the two-litre milk bottles, and, in return for such largess, the ladies from the gardening table insist that I help myself to cuttings.

And so it is that, without providing a single tree, I come away from Cannon's Creek laden down with cuttings: among them a prized climbing white ivy geranium and an elegant little daisy; all potted up in precious potting mix in little yoghurt containers for my Karori garden.

Next day, I'm back. The tenants are still out, but I unlock the car doors long enough to go and chat with the neighbour in the next unit, David Hana. He has some mates around today using his gear to shave their heads, each careful not to mess up his spotless house-keeping: Hana has custody of his four children. Cannon's Creek has always been like a geographical revolving door, but Hana reports that the neighbours have been there about three years. Sometimes they do his lawns, sometimes he does theirs. I notice that someone in my old place has made a tiny garden and there, among the winter weeds, is a carefully placed edging, made of upside-down two-litre plastic milk bottles.

From here I can see five or six houses down the road, the state house that used to be the home of the local Plunket nurse, Mrs Critchley—Titchley, as my three-year-old brother called her. He would turn up to help her brother Danny work on his car, or march into her kitchen in his gumboots to assist her, with his vast experience of the culinary arts, to make a cake in the 'concrete mixer'. That little kid gave me a certain cachet in Cannon's Creek society. It was de rigueur for girls like me to have a sibling to stick on your hip, Maori and Polynesian-style. We took that kid everywhere; often in the old-fashioned brown canvas pushchair, which I will now confess was not built to withstand one wildly excited toddler and three giggling girls being towed behind on cardboard, racing down the steep grass bank onto the Cannon's Creek reserve.

The year my brother was killed, it was a comfort beyond words that we had shared those idyllic summer days, long ago, in Cannon's Creek. Because within two years I had been enrolled at a private girls' school, two train rides and a bus ride away, where to admit to having a little brother at all was a source of absolute mortification.

The tenants are home and suddenly I'm inside and the lounge is much smaller than I remembered; it's tiny. Everything is

Previous page: Junior and Finauga Su'a

Sina and Fa'avaoa Su'a

different: the big colourful rug on the wall with Christ the Shepherd with outstretched arms is new; the bright plastic Christmas decoration by the front door, the family portraits all over the walls, the way the chairs in the minuscule lounge are lined up around the walls so that one door is blocked. And then Fa'avaoa and Finauga Su'a invite me into the dining alcove and there it is: the shock of recognition. Their dining suite chairs, no longer brand new, are still covered with the protective plastic wrap. It is exactly the sort of thing my family used to do. At the time I thought it unbearably naff, done to embarrass me personally and offend my finer sensibilities. The average Bolivian subsistence farmer, I believed, would have more style. Now, sitting here with Fa'avaoa and Finauga, and little seven-year-old Sina, I recognise protective plastic wrap as something way up there with gardening: evidence of simple aspirational hope and of decent human values.

Finauga, in his blue overalls, talks enthusiastically about a course he is doing in computers and retail marketing. Customised service, he believes, is the future. He and Fa'avaoa arrived here from Samoa in 1983. Finauga worked at Mitsubishi Motors, before it closed, and was a foreman at Firth, before it, too, closed last year. He used to get his workers on site at 5.30 a.m. and make them a cup of tea, so they would be awake and fresh for the 6.00 a.m. start. You have to be proactive, he says. He buys the newspaper once a week to check job advertisements—and he's often off, as far away as Rongotai, knocking on doors. He tells the four children that he'll have a job by Christmas. His wife's part-time night cleaning job has gone—the council contract expired—and she is now doing part-time training at the Elsdon childcare centre. But the children need security and stability, says Finauga, and 'you only get that with a permanent job. I will never give up looking.'

Fa'avaoa, a jasmine flower stuck behind her ear—yes, she would love some trees to plant—makes me coffee. Only they've run out of milk. Sina shows me her four Books in Homes books; the only books I see in the house. She snuggles beside me; her Russell School certificate for mastery of essential spelling right above the mantelpiece. She's proud of being a 'good knower'. Over in the Cannon's Creek library, her brother Junior's mates ask for the WWF magazine. World Wildlife Fund magazine, thinks the impressed librarian. It turns out it's the World Wrestling Federation mag they want. It does feature the odd complete sentence.

I tour the house. Back then, there was one toilet for eight of us and, judging by the beds, there are probably as many as that staying here now at times. The bathroom is tiny—no room for a shower box or vanity: luxury, I recall, was getting to use the soap while the letters were still embossed on it. Maybe it's the cold concrete block walls in a unit that gets little sun, but the condensation can be so bad you would swear the native flower was mildew. It was in this house that I first developed asthma. But the Su'as' only health problem is Sina's seasonal eczema. Medical bills would be a problem: on income support, the family of six has $270 a week left after rent for all other expenses.

The unit is well maintained by Housing New Zealand, although 5000 units around the country do not meet acceptable standards. The rent here is $140 a week—just under market rates. Fa'avaoa has made bright curtains. The Su'as report no burglaries, no violent crime. I have a vivid memory of the Christmas Eve the ambulance driver in the next unit—I would have sworn he was Lorne Greene from *Bonanza*—went berserk in a fit of jealous rage and caused a terrifying amount of damage with broken glass, mainly to himself. Despite the perceptions of moral decay in Cannon's

Sina shows me her four Books in Homes books; the only books I see in the house.

Creek, it was in Khandallah that our later neighbour nearly killed her partner with a hammer.

The Su'as have applied for a stand-alone house. But they like this neighbourhood. Just tonight the *Evening Post* will feature front-page evidence of the can-do spirit round here: the Aotea College senior girls' basketball team has won the Wellington secondary schools championship despite having to coach themselves. Last year, 24 students from the college received A and B Bursaries and eight others achieved subject Scholarship passes. In the 97 Enterprise NZ examinations—authorised by Oxford University—Aotea students achieved a 100 per cent pass rate (the national rate was 76 per cent).

Just weeks ago, I attended the 21st birthday of Lane Felise, a former Aotea student now majoring in business studies. The 'tight five'—the aunties from the East Coast—sang an emotional version of 'You Are Not Alone' for their nephew, the first child in his Porirua family to go to university, the first even to have a 21st party. Felise's burly Postbank boss declared the speeches to be so moving that he was 'going to have to get up and kiss him'. And that's before Felise called his parents up and gave them—as he did his older brother and sister—a present to thank them for what they have gone without so that Felise could have these opportunities.

I feel like planting another tree.

Walk on the Wild Side

james griffin
photographer: jane ussher
22 june 2002

For eight weeks, for reasons of work, I walked one of the truly great walks of New Zealand. This is not your Milford or your Routeburn. This does not require boots and packs and copious amounts of scroggin. This is the Karangahape Rd, Sunday morning, between 8.00 and 8.30 a.m. walk. From sin to salvation.

K Rd has, let's face it, been eulogised to death. Be it the beating heart (and other organs) of Auckland's sleaze industry, or the vibrant thoroughfare that encapsulates all that is good and fine and multicultural about Polynesia's largest city, or simply a prick of a road to drive down at 5.00 p.m. Friday, the old darling has about as much character as is possible to cram into a kilometre and change of shabby-but-in-a-nice way inner-city architecture.

I have, of course, walked the Karangahape Rd walk many times before. I've done the weekend cafe/shopping stroll and the 2.00 a.m. nightclub stumble and the early evening 'can I make it home before it starts raining again?' hustle, but to truly appreciate the many faces of K Rd, to watch it wake up or go to sleep or decide 'bugger it, let's keep partying', I would heartily recommend the Sunday morning, 8.00–8.30 a.m. ramble.

You approach from the west, from Ponsonby Rd, where the first lattes of the day are hitting the first tables to the first mutterings of 'I'm sure the *Sunday Star-Times* used to be better than this'. The sun is in your eyes. Or, on a true Auckland day, the sun then the rain then the sun again, is in your eyes.

You cut across the forecourt of the Caltex station, onto K Rd proper, to be greeted by the mating cry of the first of the local wildlife.

'Hey ba-a-a-aby. Looking for some company?'

Not wishing to denigrate the venerable profession of streetwalking, but few things are sadder than a lone prostitute plying her trade by daylight. The Alliance Party or

How's Life?, maybe. In truth this only happened once and I averted my eyes, muttered a polite 'thank you, no' and scurried on. I'm sure it was coincidence that she stood across from the Telecom building, not that she was a management casualty whose golden parachute had failed.

But this lady of the night (and breakfast) is K Rd's very own Statue of Liberty, welcoming travellers to the Land of the Free. Or, in this case, the Land of Pay for It, as we pass the massage parlours that keep the K Rd tradition alive long after all the others slithered off down to Fort St. There are plenty of sandwich boards, inviting punters inside, but in the eight weeks of my walking I saw nary a coming or a going. I guess 8.15 on a Sunday morning isn't exactly rush hour in the massage business.

Also not exactly rushing are the survivors reclining on the bench seats under the bus shelter over the motorway. At least I always presumed they were survivors, even though there were few signs of life. And when I say 'reclining', l mean reclining. I guess the ability to sleep in public with one's mouth wide open and drool hanging from one's chin is directly proportionate to the amount of alcohol consumed. Alcohol—the effects thereof—is something of a theme on the K Rd Sunday walk.

As is, when it comes to the bus shelter, the complete absence of buses. In the eight weeks I took this walk, I do not recall seeing one. I'm sure this was simply my schedule failing to coincide with that of Auckland's public transport providers. At 8.31 or thereabouts, I imagine the street is clogged with big yellow buses, their cheerful drivers happily assisting the comatose on board and whisking them off to wherever they desire to be whisked.

The source of this human debris is, of course, K Rd's many bars. And, thanks to New Zealand's enlightened licensing laws, allowing people to drink and gamble pretty much whenever they like, some of these bars are open at 8.20 on

Not that I judge those who drink at this hour . . . but beer for breakfast I'm sure is not recommended by the Heart Foundation.

Sunday morning. Not that I judge those who drink at this hour—they may be shift workers, popping in for a quick one on their way home—but beer for breakfast I'm sure is not recommended by the Heart Foundation. On the other hand, walking through a group of people clutching Steinlager bottles and speaking gibberish, the international language of the drunk, is enough to get my heart pumping. It's the adrenalin rush of not knowing whether they're about to bottle you, hug you, ask you for money or enquire after the next bus.

'I'm sure at 8.31 a fleet of them will come around the corner.'

'That's good, because I've been standing outside this bar since midnight.'

'There's a spare bench in the bus shelter if you want a nap while you're waiting.'

'What a fine idea. Beer?'

And if the conversation were not that civil I'm sure the gaggle of bouncers standing by the kerb, comparing how far they threw drunks the night before ('Six metres, straight into a rubbish bin, I swear') would come to my aid. But, to be on the safe side, I avoid eye contact and move on.

And the most godawful noise assails my ears. Dance music in all its infernal glory, spewing forth from Staircase as it disgorges its young things in their uniforms of tank-tops and trainers, little mid-riff tops and low-slung jeans. They're all extremely perky as they hug each other and text their friends trapped inside. How do these young people stay awake all night and emerge into the daylight full of love? It must be something in the water.

Around the bend and it's all downhill. Literally, not metaphorically, because the wildlife here is just as interesting. Men and women covered in Italian advertising slogans whiz past on bicycles, brightly coloured condoms on wheels. Members of Auckland's itinerant bewildered population sit on benches, striking up their first imaginary conversation of the day. Council workers peer down manholes and spray-paint strange hieroglyphics on the footpath. Those who have survived the tyranny of bad techno music take refuge in caffeine and bad ambient music. The sinners of the city stand discussing the options—drink more or collapse.

But as Queen St, and the point where I leave K Rd, hoves into view, salvation is at hand. Families. Nicely dressed couples with their nicely dressed children disembark from their cars to walk around the corner to the Baptist Tabernacle. They toddle off to be saved as I toddle off to earn a crust.

One morning, at the beginning of the K Rd walk, as I strode manfully past Ponsonby's Reservoir bar, wishing I hadn't had that last glass of pinot gris the night before, I had to step over a used hypodermic needle. I'd like to think it fell from the purse of an insulin user, but in reality the *Truth* headlines screamed in my head—'K RD DRUG SHOCK HORROR!' It was a sad thing to encounter on a beautiful Auckland morning, but then isn't the beauty of K Rd that it runs the whole length of humanity?

Or, as one might say to those heading off to pray for the rest of us—hey, you gotta sin to be saved.

How the West Was Won

bruce ansley
photographer: jane ussher
24 august 2002

Battered and bruised by years of economic reform and re-form, the West Coast has boomed back with record growth and renewed energy. What's driving this new gold rush?

Suddenly the West Coast is looking good. The most downtrodden of regions, the most celebrated, pitied, lauded and mocked, is getting itself a new life. The odds are turning its way at last.

This is such a *different* place. If you drive from Wellington to Auckland, you cover the length of the West Coast but get none of its variety. Abrupt cliffs, gorges, rivers that rise from the ground and as quickly disappear, vast estuaries, spectral caverns and everywhere the relics of its people who have pecked a living here since long before the first Pakeha began killing seals in the late 18th century.

People in the north of the Coast resemble Aucklanders and their Bombay Hills. They believe the place is only habitable north of Barrytown, where it's warmer although no less wet; there's nothing fabled about West Coast rain. Down south the legends live: Ross, in the centre of a rich old goldfield, is called the billion-dollar town because that is how much gold is said to lie under its streets.

Only 30,302 people live in this long, long stretch of country. It is hardly surprising that the Coast is so elusive that not even its own people have it pinned down.

A message on my desk complains about Austin Mitchell's *Pavlova Paradise Revisited* on TV. The writer, a Coaster, says he is sick of being painted quirky, quaint and almost extinct.

That is a common cause on the Coast. But locals are divided on the way to beat the cliche. Some want the place ironed out, de-kinked, Rotaried-up, tidied into a corporate-progressive model. Others want it appreciated for what it is. The Coast is full of a weird, unfocused energy.

A famous story tells of a party of sealers captured by Maori in the deepest south and marched north as the Coast's first takeaway dinners. One or two managed to excuse themselves from the table and escape to tell the tale.

It is a West Coast parable.

Coasters have made their living on one essential principle: if it is there for the taking, take it. Coal, gold and timber have all had their time in the sun. But the big three are now tourism, farming (especially dairying) and mining. Forestry is close behind.

There is an immediate tension. The huge new Pike River coal mine cannot go ahead until the government says it can get access across a pocket of conservation land. Limiting the size of the Macraes gold mine near Reefton, bang in the middle of a conservation estate, was seen by Coasters as a betrayal. Ending the felling of rimu forest and nobbling Timberlands' plans to log beech caused such upset that there is a marked lack of contempt for a Dobson man charged last week with stealing rimu trees from public land—the third case of theft of now very valuable native trees.

Former Conservation Minister Sandra Lee is reviled for creating, in her last hours in office, 77,500 ha of new wilderness areas. PM Helen Clark called the rabid end of the pro-logging lobby 'feral'. But the West Coast sees itself penned by cosseted green cityfolk who have no right to tell them anything about 'their' resources.

The final verdict on plundering for a living has been economic. The reforms of the 80s and 90s hit the Coast hard. It lost a quarter of its population as jobs in the mines disappeared, government work shrivelled and local industry flew. Here they like Jim Anderton for his regional development policies almost as much as they loathed Sandra Lee.

Now the numbers are turning the Coast's way. The sensors are picking up a sea change here on the shores of the Tasman Sea. A new study from Business and Economic Research Ltd (Berl) shows that a single earner on $40,000 in an average suburban house on the Coast is much better off than a person in the same situation in Auckland—after tax and mortgage, the Coaster will still have $24,700 in their pocket, compared with a paltry $3900 in Auckland or $10,800 in Wellington. A Coast household with two earners pulling in $65,000 will have $47,500 left compared with $26,800 in Auckland.

Certainly this is basic work, says Berl's Kel Sanderson. But the fact remains that you can live here, in a warm, wet climate such as Auckland's, for a fraction of the price. And you can go to the gym for $5, the movies for $9.

The Coast is delighted to announce that a rising number of people are moving over the hill—their way.

Last year economic growth was running at almost twice the national average, according to National Bank figures (second only to Southland, another dairy-boom zone). This year growth is down—but only to the national average.

When the government effectively shut down the native forest logging industry, it gave the Coast $120m, $28m to the four local councils and the rest to promote economic development. That money is administered by the West Coast

Development Trust, which in only a year reckons the loans to new business are worth 120 jobs, have retained another 31 and will create another 370 downstream. In the next decade it aims to push the population up a third to 40,000.

Tourism is roaring ahead here. Visitor numbers jumped 20 per cent last year. Every shut-down hardware store and dairy has become a cafe, every old pub a backpackers.

Farming, especially dairying, has created a new breed on the West Coast—millionaires. Mining is big again, with the new GRD Macraes gold mine near Reefton and the Pike River mine projected to produce one million tonnes of coal a year and employ 224 people.

Unusually there are already more jobs here than workers to fill them.

Greymouth's South Beach: big new houses are being built here, looking over the Tasman Sea.

The unemployment rate is the lowest in the country. Ask the boys from Buller.

They're packing down on a ground at Westport that is also the racecourse. It is an August night, but warm enough for T-shirts. They're a man or two short in this third division team, just pipped at the post for a semi-final slot last year.

The Buller Rugby Union came up with a novel scheme this year. They advertised in city newspapers. You play rugby for Buller and get a job thrown in.

No one replied. Not so much as a solitary loosie.

Coach Grant James is a Coaster born and bred. He is married, with two children, has a good job as an engineer and lives in a nice house. Once he was surrounded by players in jobs and good homes. They left as jobs disappeared.

Now there's competition, not for jobs but from employers offering them. Tourism hot spots such as the glaciers and Punakaiki's pancake rocks, where a new tourist hotel hangs over the beach, ran badly short of staff last season. The building and construction industries need skilled people. It will get serious when the big new mines start up: Pike River needs 224 people, ranging from accountants to geologists.

Every dog has its day. The West Coast's may be coming.

Greymouth now has outside dining. They passed a special bylaw allowing it. The first cafe has set up its tables on the pavement. The first McDonald's is arriving soon and the place already has a Warehouse. There's an Irish bar and an Indian restaurant. They're preparing to pull down nice old buildings and redevelop. All the accoutrements of a city.

And here's Sam Neill, the actor, cruising up and down the Coast in his Mini Cooper while shooting Gaylene Preston's *Perfect Strangers*. Nothing like a few stars and a film crew to make a place feel cosmopolitan.

You drive from the Kumara Junction, where the coast road joins the highway, over the Main Divide, pass through flat land and look out for trains on the Taramakau Bridge. The famous bridge, its single lane carrying both cars and trains for the last 115 years, is to be modernised. A new two-lane road bridge will be built nearby. Another sign of the times.

The flashest part of Greymouth, the Coast's biggest town, is just outside it. The big new houses are built here, looking over the Tasman Sea. On a clear day Mt Cook rises nobly to the south, white peaks glowing above the sea-mist.

Tony and Maria Williams live here. It's a nice house in a nice place.

The Williamses have prospered on the Coast in a mix of its top industries. Tony Williams started as a contractor, taking over the family business. They bought the Hotel Ashley an hour before I checked in. Previously, they had owned Greymouth's other big tourist hotel, the high-rise Kings, winning a Tourism New Zealand award for its accommodation. The Williams group of companies now deals in property, tourism, farming and gold mining—they have their own gold mine on their 200 ha farm, carefully restoring the land to high-quality pasture.

They are comfortably, reassuringly affluent. They don't like saying so ('the Coast is very small'), but his BMW 4WD and her Range Rover are dead giveaways. They have just returned from Paris. Two of their three sons go to boarding school in Christchurch, and the third will too when he is old enough. They have a second house in the heart of Fendalton in Christchurch and a third on the shores of nearby Lake Brunner, where the family waterski behind their new boat.

Tony is from Greymouth, Maria from Hokitika. They are local people who have done well by staying on the West Coast. 'The West Coast has always treated us well,' says Tony. 'We like living here. The kids love it. There are a lot more opportunities here for them than there were five or 10 years ago. The obvious reason for living here is the weather. It's fantastic. Truly,' says Maria.

This is a fine house with as good a view over the swimming pool as you'd find anywhere, and heaps better than most. Local real estate agent Frank O'Donnell reckons that you'd pay $450,000 for a house similar to this. By Auckland, Wellington and even Christchurch standards, that's peanuts for this kind of luxury.

Take it from Hugh Pavletich: the West Coast is about to see its first property boom. Pavletich and his wife Margaret are Christchurch property developers who hit town a decade ago and set about changing the skyline.

The name of Pavletich crops up often when you talk to people in Greymouth. The business district there is Maori-owned through the Mawhera Incorporation, although fewer than eight per cent of the district are Maori. The land is leased to its users; and as Mawhera emerged from a peppercorn era into a world of commercial rents and a city craving development, the Pavletiches became the medium. They have built retail developments, office blocks, industrial developments. The Pavletiches introduced the Warehouse to the West Coast. They are planning further developments on the old railway yards at the back of the city.

Pavletich is from out of town, not an accepted credential on the Coast. Locals accuse him of bowling historic landmarks to make way for his developments—the 90-year-old Post Office and the equally venerable Uniting Church, both with top heritage listings, the old iron footbridge across the railway. The beautiful Customs House, built in 1906, seemed doomed to become a car park. Locals are trying to save it. Pavletich gives it the developer's kiss of doom. 'We're trying to find a commercial solution for it,' he says smoothly.

It all sounds rather like the US solution to Vietnam's problems, destroying the village in order to save it. But even when the developers are not involved, they get the blame. Tim Birchfield makes furniture with a booming sideline in selling props for films. He works out of what he reckons is the West Coast's oldest shop, a tiny cave of a place full of vague shapes with dusty hand tools hung up at the back. He shows me an organ that he reckons was once owned by 'King Dick' Seddon. He's being thrown out of his shop (although not before digging up the floor and finding an 1846 whaler's bottle). He blames developers, but the council reckons it is unsafe.

Hugh Pavletich's best guess is that he is onto a good thing. 'The Coast has been mistakenly underrated for too long,' he says. 'All of the sectors in its economy are performing well. More importantly, in my view, it's a very attractive environment for people to live in and lifestyle is becoming very important as we become more affluent. My judgement is that the West Coast is going to be increasingly recognised as a desirable place to live because of its lifestyle opportunities. We're prepared to put money on it.'

There is not an empty shop in town, and the Coast is running out of houses, too. Over here, $180,000–$250,000 buys a lot of house—an excellent house in Greymouth, for example, although in nearby Rununga, or in Reefton, you can pick up a home for as little as $30,000. Or you can buy 83 ha of bush with two waterfalls overlooking the Taramakau for $90,000. Or a cottage, 4 ha of land and a pine forest, with a permit to take some rimu on the property, for $49,000.

According to Frank O'Donnell, there just aren't enough good houses to go round due to an influx of new people—what he refers to as a 'groundswell of interest'.

The groundswell turns roller along the coast.

A single earner on $40,000 in an average suburban house on the Coast is much better off than an Aucklander or Wellingtonian in the same situation.

North of Greymouth tiny baches hang on for all they're worth to the cliffs above the sea. They say a lot about the Coasters' love of their own country and disregard for rules, although the Buller District Council wants them to get legal or go.

Along this coast and south towards the Franz Josef and Fox glaciers, prices have doubled in the past two years. 'There was a rundown property at Rapahoe [a comparatively undistinguished coastline just north of Greymouth], tin weatherboarding, past its use-by date, bulldozer material. Someone from Christchurch came across in a helicopter and paid $105,000 for it,' marvels O'Donnell. 'I've never seen so many people begging us for a slice of coast'.

The streets, like London's, were once said to be paved with gold. For some Coasters money still grows on trees, like the moss they collect and sell, or maybe even lies on beaches. But even the Coast is recognising the universal demands of environment.

The first I saw of Marty Sullivan was his profile staring out of his 4WD like a blunt instrument. I assumed he was escaping, because it was 10 minutes before our scheduled appointment. He did not answer his telephones or return messages. So much for the Coast's latest entrepreneur, I thought.

Sullivan's is the story of the stone picker and his enemies. It is peculiarly West Coast.

Currently Aucklanders are making neat little stone

Currently Aucklanders are making neat little stone gardens around their houses. It's the fashion, marvel Coasters, dopey eh.

gardens around their houses. It's the fashion, marvel Coasters, dopey eh. They want the kind of stones spat from quartz reefs, tumbled smooth by fast rivers and cast upon beaches pink and green and white and palest grey, flat and round.

The West Coast has lots of those stones on its beaches. Coasters are allowed to take small quantities for their drives and gardens, but with Aucklanders paying so much for them the stones have become a profitable sideline, like whitebaiting.

Then stone picking turned industrial. Companies are lining up for resource consents, but Sullivan actually got his. He was set to become king of the stone pickers.

Sullivan did it properly. He went to the West Coast Regional Council, the Buller District Council and even the Department of Conservation and he came away with all the proper consents nicely stamped declaring that he, Sullivan, could take 800 tonnes of stones along 40 km of superb beaches north of Westport where the Tasman foams. Then he hired a gang of stonies and went picking. At $500 a tonne he estimates that his contract is worth $2m over the five years he is allowed to collect the stones. The new stone age pays well.

But the Tasman and the locals foamed alike.

These beaches are erosion prone, they said, producing reams of official reports in support.

David Bridger first spied Sullivan and his gang of pickers. Bridger is the son of the poet Bub, who lives in nearby Granity. He owns a backpackers' hostel, the Old Slaughterhouse, high on the hills above the beach.

'Up here in my eagle's nest I saw him coming and I got down there as quick as he did.'

A fine old stand-off on the beach followed between the stone pickers and their enemies. Constable Craig Ticklepenny attended from Granity. Trespass notices were issued by the council. ('Not worth the paper they're written on,' says Sullivan.

'Not worth a tin of snow,' says Bridger.) Sullivan was ordered off by an abatement notice from the Buller District Council.

But wait a moment, wasn't that the same council that said he *could* do it? Even that it was 'happy to give approval'? Yes, but that graunching sound is the district and regional councils hitting reverse gear, or 'taking a closer look', as one put it. That's a major step for local authorities here, although it may say only that Sullivan is minor league. Sullivan is now planning his case to the Environment Court.

The conflict here is not traditional West Coast conservatives versus greens. It's as much a clash over which direction is progress. The old ways versus the new.

So I drive up that wonderful coast to Granity, where old miners' cottages line the beach, each with a door, a porch and two windows like a child's painting.

John and Anne Crawford have a potters' studio here. They oppose Marty Sullivan. 'We have people's homes endangered,' says John. 'And our heritage. Why is a place called Granity when he wants to take all the stones? No one is going to make a film here if beaches are eroded. These are Third World jobs. Perfectly good human beings reduced to picking stones off the beach. Why aren't they apprentice carpenters and plumbers? And they don't do anything with them. They send them to Auckland and Aucklanders put them in their gardens. Then what? Their wheelie-bins aren't big enough.'

The Crawfords are successful potters who bought a house a stone's throw from the Tasman for just $3000 in 1973 and made it into a good business.

Sullivan is an entrepreneur, a trader West Coast style. He runs a fruit and vege shop. The week I spoke to him he had just bought a load of steel pipe from a southern freezing works, for re-sale. He tried to charge the *Listener* for his picture, although God knows he's no oil painting.

Superficially, the traditional Coaster making his living in the old way, he is the odd man out here. Now he has to fight not just locals but local authorities trying to find a way out of the situation that they blundered into. But Sullivan's reaction is traditional enough: 'They're *all* f***ed up.'

Although not a profane man by nature, Ben Kemp is saying much the same thing. The new juggernauts are beginning to clash. On the shores of lovely Lake Brunner, Kemp, making his way in the burgeoning tourist industry, fastens a leery eye on his farming neighbours.

Kemp is a fishing guide who takes wealthy clients—doctors from the United Kingdom and the United States, Japanese businessmen, Canadian farmers—on trips costing them $600 each a day.

The farmers are dairying, a business that has made more millionaires on the Coast than gold ever did.

Previously, Kemp was an IT consultant to local government. The stress got to him. After a heart attack and a quadruple bypass, he decided he needed a better vocation, like fishing. 'It's a very enjoyable way of spending the time.'

Sullivan is an entrepreneur, a trader West Coast style . . . He tried to charge the *Listener* for his picture, although God knows he's no oil painting.

Enterprise on the shores of Lake Brunner.

So he returned to the place where he was born. He built a nice new house on Lake Brunner and he is building a couple of holiday units next door. He turned his nearby great grandmother's house into a B&B. His business is prospering.

But Kemp has been noticing a change—a singular lack of fish in rivers that had been swarming with them. The fish, he says, are disappearing. Kemp takes me down to Iveagh Bay, where expensive holiday houses are being built in a new subdivision by wealthy outsiders, mainly from Christchurch.

He points out dying stands of kahikatea around the fringes of this great lake beneath the mountains. He shows photographs of lumps of brown algae looking like floating cowpats. In fact, cows are the cause, he says. Rivers and streams are unfenced. Dairy farmers are running their stock unchecked, pumping their effluent into pristine streams and creeks. He accuses one farmer of putting a wintering pad for his cows right on the riverbed: 'The river was so full of rotting cow manure and urine that for 300 m downstream you couldn't see the colour of the stones on the river bottom. For 5 km downstream there wasn't a fish for the entire summer. Basically, it destroyed the river.'

Could this be happening on the pristine West Coast? Kemp believed so. He began collecting evidence into a damning report ('having worked in local government, I knew that the last thing they wanted was publicity'). That report was applauded by anglers from all over the country.

He says the West Coast Regional Council is letting dairy farmers get away with murder, and Fish and Game West Coast agrees. Last year there were 359 complaints about pollution and a year on 151 have still to be investigated. Chris Tonkin, Fish and Game's manager, claims that it has nothing to do with resources and everything to do with the fact that the council is dominated by dairy farmers.

But Terry Day, the council's chief executive, is sticking with the lack of resources story. Helping mates on the farms? 'That's a political question I won't answer.' John Clayton, the council's dairy farmer chair, tots up the figures: the Coast's 380 dairy farmers earn $121.6m in milk solids a year. The council is doing its best, he soothes. 'There's no reason dairying should be degrading the environment as long as they don't come in with a sledgehammer overnight. You can't have an environmental policeman in every paddock.'

A Coast-like postscript to this episode. Kemp's picture was published in local newspapers. Rauhine Lilley in Hokitika recognised the name. She had been searching for Kemp for many years. He was her long-lost father. She gained a father, Kemp another five grandchildren.

West Coast local authorities have always been, ah, eccentric. One Greymouth mayor even threatened to move the entire city upriver when the Maori landowners began pushing for commercial rates to replace the existing peppercorn rentals.

With the pressure on and money in their pockets, the Hokitika-based Westland District Council is demonstrating its unique brand of speed wobble.

It has embraced a company that claims to have the secrets of producing a new wonder plastic. The council has lent the company, FT Manufacturing, $500,000 and is providing a new $2.2m factory.

Sleuthing by the Christchurch *Press* then discovered that the company principal, Soren Kierkegaard (he changed his name by deed poll to that of the Danish philosopher), had not had any machinery nor product, only a promise of good things to come. The *Press* obtained a secret copy of a report by Deloitte Touche Tohmatsu, which found the venture high-risk and unsubstantiated. The report was not shown to councillors.

John Drylie, lawyer turned Presbyterian minister and now Westland Mayor, is quite happy about all of this. 'It'll be good news for the district.' But isn't it a bit of a punt? 'From the outside it may appear that way. But from the inside it has been very closely analysed.'

The Auditor-General's office is investigating aspects of the way the council handled the deal.

And Maureen Pugh, Westland's only woman councillor, reckons it's crook. 'Just when our reputation is looking more positive, something like this comes along and sets the West Coast back. It's an extreme gamble. I've spent many hours researching these people and the more I learn the riskier it sounds.'

Then again, the West Coast was founded on risk. *Plus ça change, plus c'est la meme chose.*

End of the Road

b r u c e   a n s l e y

p h o t o g r a p h e r :   j o h n   m c c o m b i e

2 2   m a y   2 0 0 4

The road dies at Lake Taylor. Expires, despite a sign 30 km back saying it went all the way to Loch Katrine. The track taking its place wouldn't make a road even a century and a half ago when they were bashing a way through this North Canterbury back country, over Harpers Pass to the West Coast.

The road builders had only pack mules and their own two feet. The *Listener* is equipped with the latest in new-millennium technology, a white Suzuki. And the sky is blue. A sweet smell of rosehips wafts on the breeze. Golden tussock drips into a silver lake. It's so beguiling that we open the gate at Lake Taylor and drive right on through.

The road immediately becomes a morass. Holes turn into puddles, then craters. The car bucks like a mule sensing disaster.

The puddles grow bigger and browner until we come to one so wide, so turgid, that I am thankful for the car's compass. The cutting edge of technology voyages to the middle, then baulks. Investigative journalism takes a plunge.

We sit for a moment. The ripples die. Beech forest ahead, refuge behind. The car chooses retreat and reverses obligingly. From here, we walk. It's a long, lumpy way. At the end lie the Loch Katrine baches.

What is left of them.

For the Department of Conservation (DoC) decided that the settlement of 60 baches should go, sacrificed to a principle that Peter Lawless, its acting policy manager, puts like this: 'We should not have private buildings not open to public access on public land.'

But public access to Loch Katrine is already bad. In the course of a day, I saw only two other vehicles on the road. At the lake itself, the competition for space is hardly fierce. Katrine is the smallest of four lakes huddling here below the Southern Alps. Big lakes, small crowd.

Held together with everything from baling twine to No 8 wire, the iconic and much-loved Kiwi bach is pure Kiwiana, with many occupying Conservation Department land—but not for much longer if the department has its way.

A fisherman's jetty on the
Selwyn River.

Is the principle worth the loss of a community?

The bach settlement here grew up over more than half a century. They were the usual Kiwi baches, built from whatever was handy, oddly practical, sometimes quaint.

Rob Stanley, a bach owner, mourns the loss. 'It's not about ownership or money,' he says. 'It's about values, giving families the opportunity to bring their children up in an environment totally different from the one they live in, one very much part of our common heritage. That's at least as important as the concerns of some over-zealous environmentalists.'

If you ask what harm the baches were doing, except for getting in the way of a principle, the answer is none at all. Even their arch-enemies, Forest & Bird, support DoC's stance, but concede a point: 'In some cases, human habitation is a good idea,' says the society's Canterbury field officer, Tony Lockwood.

'The settlement was a bit of classic Kiwiana,' says Katrine bach owner David Kirkness. 'Lots of people camped there *because* of the community, and if they didn't like it, there's a hell of a lot of country around these lakes. Settlements like this provide a public good. This is where people learn conservation values. Rather than excluding people, DoC should be trying to encourage them.'

DoC counters that perhaps more people will visit the lake now that they have knocked out a deal with Loch Katrine bach owners. The baches would go, and their owners would pay for 10 sanitised new ones built to regulation and available to the public for hire. DoC cites this as a good, negotiated solution.

Was Kirkness happy with the deal? 'No,' he says. 'But what do you do when the government takes a bulldozer to you?'

Must all Kiwi baches on conservation estate go?

Since DoC announced that its new policy would harden its previous resolve to terminate private occupation—baches—

on the third of the country it controls, several hundred bach owners across the country have been trembling around their Tilley lamps: from Whangaruru and Pahi in Northland to Tongaporutu and Kaupokonui in Taranaki, the Orongo-rongos and Ocean Beach at the bottom of the North Island to Nelson's Boulder Bank, in the three big bach settlements that make Canterbury the most-affected region, or the West Coast's Big Bay to Otago's tiny Nevis or Skippers Creek or Bruce Rocks.

With few outside Forest & Bird applauding its plan, and an unlikely axis of National and the Greens actively opposing it, DoC is trying to be conciliatory.

Yes, they recognise that the bach is an endangered species, they acknowledge its role in history and culture, they are prepared to negotiate and, no, they won't give anyone the straight heave. The department has more nous, they say: it will *always* negotiate.

In fact, they say, people in settlements like Lake Alexandrina, near Lake Tekapo, or the Lower Selwyn huts— a cluster of pretty, usually tiny baches wedged alongside the Selwyn River as it runs into Lake Ellesmere near Christchurch—may even have something approaching permanence.

Alexandrina is a narrow lake in the mountains, with the Two Thumbs Range glittering away to the east and the unbelievably corny, blue Tekapo to its side. Anglers love it. They began building huts there in the 1940s. Now the lake is home to some superb bach architecture and a community of about 120 huts.

Both Alexandrina and the Lower Selwyn huts are to get leases, although, according to DoC, the owners will never win freehold. Says Jim Underdown, a veteran Alexandrina negotiator: 'This is *magnificent*.'

So, why do some bach settlements get the flick while Alexandrina and Lower Selwyn get to stay?

The sound of shuffling is quite distinct. Evidently, it is all about administration, and the land's status (for all conservation land is not alike), and there were existing arrangements that DoC didn't know about when it framed its draft general policy, and anyway the new policy will *allow* flexibility.

'It allows discretion for local managers,' explains Lawless. 'Generally, public land is not available for private dwellings, but there are some exceptions. Where there's a historical situation that has to be taken into account, we don't want to set up this policy to be a nonsense: we have to take account of those special circumstances that come to light.'

So, Alexandrina has special circumstances, but, despite the extensive documentation of its bach owners, Katrine does not and the fact, for example, that Alexandrina has two judges as bach owners to Katrine's nil makes no difference at all.

Does DoC recognise any architectural or iconic status in the baches? 'Some of them do,' says Lawless cautiously, 'and Rangitoto gives a clue about how we deal with them.' The survivors of Rangitoto Island's picturesque baches are being refurbished—to the building code, anathema for the connoisseur—and rented to the public.

'The New Zealand bach has a presence in people's minds,' says Lawless. 'It's a significant part of our identity. But there's no problem with people having their baches on their own land.'

Kirkness retorts: 'The ordinary Joe can't expect now to have the classic Kiwi bach, even on the West Coast. A large slice of Kiwi society is cut off from that experience by the real-estate boom.'

Most bach owners recognise that occupying public land is a privilege, and as a result most are model citizens; they don't create mess, get in the public's way nor on its goat. Most, too, believe they are better off because their places are worth next to nothing: they value their tenure more, are freed from the

'The ordinary Joe can't expect now to have the classic Kiwi bach . . . A large slice of Kiwi society is cut off from that experience by the real-estate boom.'

dreary mull of property prices, stay clear of the envy cycle.

So, owners of 28 baches clinging Seuss-like to the precipices and wild beaches of the West Coast found themselves with a mixed blessing when the local council gave them 35-year leases.

Those baches occupied road reserve rather than conservation land, but some locals claimed that they had been turned into millionaires, courtesy of public land and a public body.

'Millionaires? A load of crap,' snorts Mac McKenzie, who owns three of the much-photographed baches. Gary Murphy, the district council's chief executive, agrees, if more politely. 'They can maintain their baches, but they can't add another storey, or even a deck,' he says. 'They have a small footprint and no security of tenure [when their leases expire].' Freehold-savvy New Zealanders are unlikely to rush them with open cheque-books.

Meanwhile, DoC is soon to be confronted with a society dedicated to the preservation of Kiwiana and Kiwi baches. Christchurch lawyer Ben Tothill is incensed enough by DoC's proposed policy to set up the group to fight it.

Between confusion and confrontation, the Kiwi bach may yet be preserved.

Behind the
Pink Door

bianca zander

photographer: jane ussher

3 july 2004

No, the Scarfies of Dunedin are not an endangered species, but maybe some of their flats should be under threat.

They call it the student ghetto, that grid of mean streets and dilapidated housing where the Scarfies live in North Dunedin. Castle, Dundas, Hyde, Clyde, Forth and Leith—the list of street names is short because the students are lazy. They don't want to walk for more than five minutes to get to university; and if they live elsewhere they can't pop home in between lectures for a pie or a nap.

Every year, as more and more students enrol at Otago—the roll is heading towards 20,000—more and more Scarfies try to squeeze themselves into the tiny precinct around the university, with predictable consequences. The standard of accommodation deteriorates as the old villas and settlers' cottages are stretched to splitting point—eight or 10 bedrooms plus one shared bathroom per dwelling is not uncommon—but each year the rents go up because supply exceeds demand. What used to be desirable because it was cheap is now overcrowded and overpriced. The meningitis season is fast approaching (already this year there have been 17 cases among 19- to 22-year-olds) and an outbreak in North Dunedin would be disastrous.

Take a house in Hyde St, home of the famous annual keg race. Six girls. Six bedrooms. Six rent cheques (Dunedin landlords charge a per-room rate). Last year, this house fetched $75 per bedroom; this year, it has gone up to $81 per room. Two of the bedrooms are in a plywood extension built out into the backyard. The bathroom is a box, with shower stall and sink. One corner of the lounge is the kitchen. The carpet is wrecked. We're talking way beyond slum chic, or even ghetto fabulous—if this house was anywhere else in the country, there would be talk of demolition. Here, in North Dunedin, it goes for $486 a week.

Who's paying? 'This is cheap,' says Becky Chittock, 19, whose home it is for the year. 'We were prepared to pay up to $95 [per week each], so we felt lucky to get this flat. This is good. It's not really that cold.' If $81 doesn't sound like much to pay for a roof over your head, bear in mind that the student allowance has resisted inflation, remaining at around $150 a week for the past decade.

Further up Hyde St, five guys pay $78 each for their house, up from $72 the year before. They moved out of their previous flat, in Castle St, because the rent went from $68 a week, to $89, over a two-year period.

When you're away from home for the first time, there is nothing more delightful than defying rules of sanitation. The guys' pad has food scraps as decoration and stacks of undone dishes. Behold the high-tech squalor. Between them, they own enough laptops, DVD players and XBoxes to open an appliance store. Nobody is suggesting that they should be installed in a well-appointed home, but are the critters paying too much to live in such a place? 'Yeah, but what can we do?' says Andrew Dotchin, 20, from Waiuku. 'If we don't live here, somebody else will.' His flatmate Rhett Murrah, who has been reading his political textbooks, reckons the landlords have formed an oligarchy. 'We can't fight it. As students, we have no say or power.'

'Landlords have got the market stitched up,' says Andrew Cushen, president of the Otago University Student Union. 'Landlords argue that demand exceeds supply, which they use to justify dramatic increases—jumps of $10 per room over a year. They argue that the market allows them to do it. Because the market is saturated, they get away with it. It's their monopoly.'

Cushen reckons that the landlords' greed is short-sighted and ultimately working to the detriment of the Dunedin economy. 'Student incomes are very tight—$150 a week. That's $10 a week less that the student can spend on whatever.' By whatever, he means beer.

He says that landlords divide into two camps. 'There are the ones who like to lease out reasonable quality homes. Then there are the roguish landlords who do no maintenance, who watch these grand old homes deteriorate to a shell and then bowl them over to develop townhouses. In 20 to 30 years, the entire character of the area will be lost, replaced by plywood and fibreboard constructions. It will be just stock housing, nothing compared to the old character flats that are there.'

Build ugly units and charge exorbitant rents and you attract a different kind of student—richer, blander, more likely to be from Auckland, and, according to the whisperers, more likely to be Asian.

By character flats, Cushen means villas like the Pink Pussy, over on Castle St, which has so much character that students will sign the lease before they have set eyes on it. When the list goes out each August, for properties available the following year, students have few criteria. According to Cushen, 'They want to know, "Is it in Castle St?"—Everyone wants to live there. "Will it fit my double bed? Is it the Pink

Pussy? Great, I'll take it."'

The term 'Scarfie' is thought to have been coined in the 1960s, after it was noticed that Dunedin students wore scarves constantly, because of the lack of adequate heating in their homes. Since then, the culture has been immortalised in the movie *Scarfies*, and sensationalised, annually, in documentary and news footage of orientation week. But, once upon a time, the Scarfie lifestyle was about more than how much beer you could drink before flashing your butt at a waiting TV camera. Whatever happened, for example, to intellectual idealism?

Flashback to 1988. After spending a year at Unicol, the halls of residence where first-years learn to behave badly, Swanni from Oamaru wants to go flatting. He feels institutionalised. To prepare himself, he has been staying up all night drinking coffee and smoking cigarettes, missing all his lectures and reading too much Sartre. His friend and co-philosopher of the time, Wallace Chapman, remembers: 'I told Swanni about this text I was reading called *Summerhill*, by A. S. Neill, who was an old guru in the 60s. Neill envisaged a school where kids had the freedom to be themselves, not tied up by academia, but by "true learning". Swanni and I were so impressed that we started imagining, not a Freedom School, but a Freedom Flat.' The only rule of this Freedom Flat was that there would be no rules at all.

Swanni, Wallace and five others moved into 3 Clyde St and began their social experiment. They painted the front door in homage to Pink Floyd, covering it with pink bricks like the album cover for The Wall, except that their door said, rather obviously, 'Pink Flat—The Door'. Chapman recalls, 'As viciously uncool as Pink Floyd were in 80s Dunedin—remember this was Flying Nun time—they represented a real philosophy to us.'

A room in the Freedom Flat cost $40 a week, but rent was more of a 'philosophical concept' than a hard reality. In other words, it was never paid.

'From day one it was a disaster,' says Chapman. Members of the National Front moved in, along with their two dogs, Gretchen and Adolf, and, because it was a Freedom Flat, they couldn't be kicked out. 'It all turned rather violent. Someone once pulled a sawn-off shotgun. There were three police raids. There was the council threatening us with closure.' They made international headlines when a photographer from the German magazine *Der Spiegel*, in town to do a story about Scarfies, stopped outside the flat and announced, 'I am intrigued by your Freedom Flat and the Egyptian Satanist symbols on the front fence.'

The Pink Floyd door at 3 Clyde Street is now a Dunedin landmark. Earlier this year, it was restored by the landlord, who hired a colour consultant to match the exact shade of pink. 'If only he knew it was housepaint,' says Chapman.

Behind the pink door, student life continues to be squalid. It is no longer a Freedom Flat but the home of bland commerce types, with an XBox in the lounge and a Subaru parked in the street. When they moved in, the landlord told them they could do whatever they liked to the flat, but under no circumstances were they to interfere with the front door. They refer to the pink door as though it is a trophy, a relic from the past, which makes them much cooler than their neighbours. It wouldn't occur to the kids next door, you suspect, to paint one of their own. There is a sense in North Dunedin that each successive generation of students is feeding off the mythology of the past, too dull to create its own.

Chapman still has the clipping from *Der Spiegel*, which shows him sporting an afro and eating a pie, next to the Pink Floyd door. They say Otago University is where you become the man you will be for the rest of your life. Chapman is now 35—works in advertising, has short hair, doesn't eat pies. He is, however, nostalgic for his Scarfie days and the disappearing culture. 'It all seemed so heady, and it all seemed so much a product of the varsity days of the 80s—the pre-student-loan days—when living, and not an education, was the goal.'

index

photographers/writers

Photographers

Writers